The Teaching of Ethics VI

The Teaching of Ethics in the Social Sciences

Donald P. Warwick

INSTITUTE OF
SOCIETY, ETHICS AND
THE LIFE
SCIENCES THE
HASTINGS
CENTER

The Hastings Center
Institute of Society, Ethics and the Life Sciences
360 Broadway
Hastings-on-Hudson, New York 10706

Library of Congress Cataloging in Publication Data

Warwick, Donald P
    The teaching of ethics in the social sciences.
    (The Teaching of ethics ; 6)
    Bibliography: p.
    1. Social sciences—Study and teaching.
    2. Ethics—Study and teaching. 3. Social sciences—
Methodology. I. Title. II. Series: Teaching
of ethics.
H62.W286   170′.7   80–10154
ISBN 0–916558–11–8

Table of Contents

Introduction vii

I.   Current Teaching 1
     A. Courses on Ethics 2
     B. Sections of Courses 5
     C. Informal Discussions 8
     D. Tributary Activities 10
     E. Goals in the Teaching of Ethics 13

II. Personal Origins of Involvement 17

III. Disciplinary Climates: Past and Present 23
     A. Early History 24
     B. The Triumph of Positivism: 1930–65 27
     C. The Return of Ethics: 1965–79 32

IV. Present Attitudes Toward Teaching 37

V.   Whither the Teaching of Ethics? 45
     A. Recommendations 48

VI. Topics and Readings 55
     A. Social Science and Society 56
     B. General Ethical Issues in Social Research ... 57
     C. Ethical Issues Arising from Specific Research
        Methods and Settings 58
     D. Applied Social Science and the Ethics of Interven-
        tion 62

Notes 63

Appendix A: Questionnaire on the Teaching of Ethics in the Social Sciences 65

Appendix B: Persons Contacted 67

FOREWORD

A concern for the ethical instruction and formation of students has always been a part of American higher education. Yet that concern has by no means been uniform or free of controversy. The centrality of moral philosophy in the undergraduate curriculum during the mid-nineteenth century gave way later during that century to the first signs of increasing specialization of the disciplines. By the middle of the twentieth century, instruction in ethics had, by and large, become confined almost exclusively to departments of philosophy and religion. Efforts to introduce ethics teaching in the professional schools and elsewhere in the university often met with indifference or outright hostility.

The past decade has seen a remarkable resurgence of interest in the teaching of ethics at both the undergraduate and professional school levels. Beginning in 1977, The Hastings Center, with the support of the Rockefeller Brothers Fund and the Carnegie Corporation of New York, undertook a systematic study of the teaching of ethics in American higher education. Our concern focused on the extent and quality of that teaching, and on the main possibilities and problems posed by widespread efforts to find a more central and significant role for ethics in the curriculum.

As part of that project, a number of papers, studies, and monographs were commissioned. Moreover, in an attempt to gain some degree of consensus, the authors of those studies worked together as a group for a period of two years. The study presented here represents one outcome of the project. We hope and believe it will be helpful for those concerned to advance and deepen the teaching of ethics in higher education.

Daniel Callahan   Sissela Bok
Project Co-Directors
The Hastings Center
Project on the Teaching of Ethics

About the Author

Donald P. Warwick

Donald P. Warwick is an Institute Fellow at the Harvard Institute for International Development. He also teaches in the Department of Sociology and in the Graduate School of Education at Harvard. He received his Ph.D. in Social Psychology from the University of Michigan and has previously taught at Oberlin College, Michigan, and York University in Toronto. He has written *A Theory of Public Bureaucracy, The Sample Survey: Theory and Practice* (with C. Lininger), and several articles on ethics and the social sciences. His current research deals with the ethics of international population programs and with program implementation in Indonesia.

Introduction

The current renaissance in the teaching of ethics has penetrated almost every field of professional training, including the social sciences. Nowhere, however, has the response been more ambivalent than in the disciplines of anthropology, sociology, and psychology. While most professionals in these fields would grant the need for some set of ethical standards, especially if couched in very broad terms, explicit teaching about ethics still generates considerable wariness and suspicion. Some say that the teaching of ethics is basically irrelevant, for the ethical questions raised by the social sciences are so trivial that they should not occupy valuable class time. In response to a questionnaire for this project, a well-known social scientist wrote: "In terms of educating social scientists to ethical issues in research then, I think the endeavor suffers from certain drawbacks: the absence of reasonably well codified ethical standards and procedures for operationalizing them, the relatively slight moral dilemmas encountered, and the limited range of ethical issues compared to those seen in fields of practice such as medicine, psychotherapy, marriage counseling, or financial advising. Social science *research* seems to me a rather barren area for the ethicists. . ." In other words, it is scarcely worthwhile teaching about the ethics of research when there is so little to teach. The same writer stated another objection shared by many social scientists: ethical behavior is best taught by example rather than in the classroom. Budding professionals will learn to be ethically responsible when their mentors espouse and observe high standards of professional conduct. Still others regard the teaching of ethics as part of the larger assault on research freedom typified by institutional review boards. And occasional comments are heard that those who incline toward the teaching of ethics are the lame and the halt of their fields, professionals who compensate for their own ineptitude in research by preaching about the scholarly sins of others. As a psychologist put it in a letter to this writer, "There is some feeling among researchers that people who focus on ethics are do gooders who don't do research anyway and so would gladly sacrifice important research questions for rather trivial technical points." The scene is shifting as larger numbers of social scientists teach courses or parts of courses on ethics, but as of 1979 this line of instruction was uncommon and an object of considerable skepticism.

In its broadest sense the teaching of ethics in the social sciences has a long and dialectical history. When sociology and anthropology were established as separate disciplines, their founders often aspired to a new science of morality. For visionaries such as August Comte, modern social science was to be not only an instrument of analysis, but a vehicle for virtue. Even Freud, who wrote in the idiom of science, could barely suppress his moral ardor for a world without repression. But over time the explicit ethical component of these disciplines eroded under pressure from professionalism, and the imperatives of science came to the fore. By the 1950s morality had become "mores" and the term "ethics" was consigned to the corners of professional practice, rarely heard and even more rarely noticed. The Code of Ethics of the American Psychological Association was duly read by students in clinical psychology, but more as a ritual to be dispensed with than a subject for serious thought. Courses on ethics in the social sciences were nonexistent, and the topic was rarely raised explicitly outside the classroom. With the advent of the student movement, the Vietnam War, Project Camelot, and public concern with research abuses, the subject began to be broached with increasing frequency, and gradually found its way into the curriculum. From the late 1960s until the present, the teaching of ethics has slowly expanded, particularly in courses on research methods. Over the past century ethics has thus moved from macro-morality, intrinsic to the discipline, to near-invisibility as a topic of discussion back to a middle ground of concern with the professions themselves.

This essay will provide an overview of the teaching of ethics in the social sciences both in historical perspective and at present. The teaching of ethics will refer to instruction involving more or less self-conscious reflection on ethical aspects of the social sciences, including theory, research, and practice. I will exclude the implicit teaching of ethics seen, for example, in the presentation of Freudian or Marxian theory. Although Freud's theory of the libido, as one instance, carried a heavy freight of ethical judgment, the straightforward presentation and analysis of this material would not meet the present criterion for the teaching of ethics. The definition would be met by a course systematically raising for inspection the ethical paradigms and value judgments running through Freudian theory. The social sciences covered here will be mainly anthropology, sociology, and psychology. Although economics, geography, and political science are also social sciences, discussions of ethics have been less common there than in the three disciplines selected for analysis. Moreover, when ethical issues are raised, they are often identical to those in anthropology, sociology, and psychology.

The following discussion is based on several sources of information. First, to determine the number, location, and approximate content of courses on ethics, I commissioned a review of about 700 college and university catalogues. Further information on courses emerged from a similar search conducted by The Hastings Center. Second, I tried to contact, in person, by mail, or by telephone, all social scientists known to be interested in the teaching of ethics or well informed about the climate for such teaching. Many were sent the brief questionnaire included in Appendix A. In the end I contacted some forty-four individuals, of whom thirty-six responded in some fashion. The list of contacts, minus one individual who asked to be dropped from the sample, is provided in Appendix B. In addition, I drew on my own experience, not only in the teaching of ethics, but as a sometime member of two departments of psychology and four departments of sociology, including the chairmanship of a large department of sociology and anthropology. Finally, I should note that the discussion is limited to the social sciences in North America. A comparable analysis carried out for Europe and Latin America would undoubtedly produce quite a different picture, including dissimilar notions of the meaning of ethics in the social sciences.

I. Current Teaching

To what extent is ethics currently being taught in the social sciences? The answer depends on precisely what is meant by teaching. Does it refer to formal courses? To informal discussions between faculty and graduate students? To conferences and colloquia only loosely related to the academic curriculum? Unfortunately, there has been some tendency to identify the teaching of ethics mainly with curricular offerings bearing that name.[1] Yet the range of activities normally included under the rubric of teaching in the social sciences is much broader. In the leading graduate programs, courses on theory, methods, and substantive fields of research are but one part of professional training. Also essential are research experience, examinations based largely on private readings, qualifying papers, and a dissertation. Beyond formal requirements, most of us would place high pedagogical value on such experiences as informal contacts with faculty and fellow students, attendance at colloquia, conferences, and professional meetings, and related extracurricular activities. The operating definition of an outstanding department, in fact, embraces the totality of formal courses, professional ethos, and informal socializing experiences. Thus, the proper paradigm for considering the teaching of ethics in the social sciences is teaching as commonly defined in those disciplines. To confine the analysis to formal courses may be to miss the most powerful kinds of exposure to ethical reflection.

For present purposes I will distinguish among four kinds of teaching about ethics. The first, most obvious, and least frequent is the regularly scheduled course dealing wholly or substantially with ethics in the social sciences. A second and more common variety is a section on ethics offered as part of a course bearing some other title, such as research methods or criminology. A third and more elusive type takes place through informal discussions between students and faculty. The prototype would be the consideration of ethics in the context of a research project involving faculty and students. Finally, the teaching of ethics might include a variety of extracurricular activities that provide the raw material for formal teaching about ethics and often have strong didactic value in themselves.

A. Courses on Ethics

In 1977 I estimated that across the United States there were probably no more than ten courses dealing mainly with ethics in the social sciences. While the number seems to have risen even between 1977 and 1979, the total is probably not over fifteen. Given the mounting activities in the less formal areas of teaching, and the growing volume of publications on ethics in the social sciences, we might well expect that number to double or triple in coming years. But for reasons to be indicated it is highly unlikely that separate courses on ethics will become a standard part of the social science curriculum by 1990.

During the 1950s there seemed to be no courses dealing with ethics in any of the major departments of anthropology, psychology, or sociology. In the early 1960s Gideon Sjoberg, a sociologist, and Herbert Kelman, a psychologist, set the stage for subsequent courses through their teaching and writing on the politics and ethics of the social sciences. Though I was not able to determine if Sjoberg offered a formal course on ethics, he was cited by several respondents as a significant influence on their thinking in this area. The book which he edited, *Ethics, Politics, and Social Research,* provided valuable raw material for teaching, and is still widely used as a source of readings.[2] Throughout the 1960s Kelman had been raising questions of ethics in his courses on social psychology and allied topics, and in 1968 he brought out *A Time to Speak*, a collection of his essays in this field.[3] In 1969 he and I teamed up to offer a graduate seminar on "Politics, Ethics, and Social Research" in the Department of Social Relations at Harvard. This attracted about twenty participants, including one faculty member from another university and an editor from Harvard University Press. During the 1960s there was also considerable debate about ethics and codes of ethics in the Society for Applied Anthropology (SAA) and its publication, *Human Organization*. One of the protagonists was Richard Adams, who pressed for explicit attention to ethics while he was president of the SAA in 1962–63. Also active then and later was Murray Wax, an anthropologist with a background in philosophy. However, until the mid-1970s courses on ethics in the social sciences were very rare.[4]

At present there are several such courses being taught, and at least one on the books which has never been taught. Florida International University in Miami is quite unusual in *requiring* a course on ethics of all majors in its Department of Sociology and Anthropology. This offering, "Ethical Issues in Social Science Research," is taught by William Osborne, Jr., and is given two to three times per academic year. It considers such questions as morality and social scientific "neutrality" and value systems influencing social scientists. For several years E.L. Pattullo of Harvard's Department of Psychology and Social Relations has offered a seminar, open to both undergraduates and graduate students, on ethical problems in behavioral research. The course is organized around *Experimentation with Human Beings*, edited by Jay Katz.[5] Pattullo notes that the course "has not elicited great interest." Very similar in focus was the graduate seminar on research ethics offered for several years by Professor Norman Hilmar in the Department of Sociology at the University of Colorado. The text was again *Experimentation with Human Beings*, supplemented by anecdotes and cases drawn from the instructor's experience in the United States Government. Following Hilmar's retirement from the department in 1977, the course was discontinued.

One of the more active persons in this field of late, both in teaching and writing, is Joan Sieber, Professor of Psychology at the California State University at Hayward. She currently offers an undergraduate course on Research Ethics in the university's General Studies program. The syllabus states:

> The purpose of this course is to sensitize students to the nature of ethical problems in research. Upon completion of this course, students are expected to be competent at evaluating research proposals (or treatment proposals, or program evaluation proposals) in terms of the ethical problems that might arise in the proposed program of work; further, students are expected to be competent at recommending ways to resolve or reduce the anticipated ethical problems.

The course text is a manuscript prepared by Sieber on ethical issues in social scientific research.

Also very active in the teaching of ethics is Myron Glazer, chairman of the Department of Sociology and Anthropology at Smith College. Author of the ethically attuned book, *The Research Adventure*, Glazer introduces ethical concerns into all of his courses.[6] One of his offerings, "Ethical Issues in Social Organizations," explores moral questions arising from medical and social science research, CIA activities, corporate decisions, and whistle-blowing. Another sociologist with strong interests in ethics is Ted Vaughan of the Department of Sociology at the University of Missouri in Columbia. In 1975 Vaughan offered a graduate seminar on "Ethics and Social Science," but has not repeated this course. Edward Diener of the Psychology Department at the University of Illinois at Urbana-Champaign also offered a graduate seminar on research ethics, but was discouraged when only one student enrolled.

Entire courses on ethics are even more rare in anthropology than in sociology or psychology. In the fall of 1978, Murray and Rosalie Wax offered a seminar on "Anthropology and Ethics" in the Department of Sociology and Anthropology at Washington University in St. Louis. The course drew one undergraduate, one graduate student, and one registered doctoral student. The instructors plan to repeat the seminar in 1979, and feel that with better publicity it might attract more students. The Catholic University of America lists a course on ethical problems in anthropology, but it has never been offered. The instructor, Conrad Reining, writes: "It is on a demand basis. While some students express an interest, the faculty has not yet seen a need for it to be taught on an exclusive basis."[7] Moving away from professional ethics, the Department of Anthropology at Stanford University offers a course on "The Ethics of Development in a Global Context." Taught by Robert Textor and Bernard Siegel, it explores the ethics of development per se rather than just the ethics of anthropologists working in developing countries.

The question of what is covered by the teaching of ethics is posed rather sharply by a course on "Experimental Design, Research, and Measurement," taught by Robert Boruch in the Psychology Department at Northwestern University. For some years, Boruch and his colleagues have been exploring concrete ways in which ethical difficulties can be avoided, resolved, or circumvented through more effective research design. In this seminar and in his writing, Boruch asks, for example, if the usual problems of confidentiality in survey research can be reduced through the technique known as randomized response methods. Instead of asking an individual to state categorically whether he has cheated on his last federal income tax return, the person is asked to report truthfully with a probability less than one. In this way estimates of the proportions of tax cheaters remain accurate, but knowledge about violations by any single individual is uncertain.[8] While these and related questions of design in Boruch's seminar arise from a concern about ethical questions such as privacy, the course content itself involves very little explicit attention to normative issues. Hence, it would be stretching the term to cite this course as an example of the teaching of ethics as such, but it would also be shortsighted to miss the strong ethical orientation behind the treatment of research methodology.

B. Sections of Courses

The most dramatic increase in teaching about ethics lies in the addition of sections on this topic to courses on mainline subjects in the social sciences. Even a decade ago it was exceptional for courses on research methods, theory construction, social psychology, or criminology to have a set of lectures and readings devoted explicitly to ethical issues. The instructor might have noted "ethical difficulties" with certain studies, such as the Milgram obedience experiments, but rarely was there a specific time and block of readings on this subject. Today there are not only several books completely devoted to ethical issues in the social sciences, but chapters on ethics are becoming a common feature of textbooks on research methods, handbooks in various substantive areas, and other sources of course readings. Whereas some of these chapters reflect mainly a strategic concern for coping with institutional review boards and other regulations, many are explicitly and seriously concerned with the moral issues at stake in theory, research, and practice. As is often the case, academic instruction has both followed and reinforced the trend in the literature. As a result there are now at least several dozen instructors in the social sciences who regularly incorporate lectures, discussions, and readings on ethics in courses given under other titles. The following are but a few examples.

Richard Adams, Professor of Anthropology at the University of Texas, includes readings and one seminar session on ethics as part of his course on "Field Methods." He also devotes half a seminar to this topic in his course on Social Anthropology, a core offering for graduate students. As is true of most discussions of ethics in anthropology, his readings place strong emphasis on the political dimensions and repercussions of anthropological research. Adams also introduces several controversial cases in his discipline, such as the study of "Springdale,"[9] the Vicos Project in Peru,[10] and Colin Turnbull's research on a mountain people.[11]

John Galliher, a sociologist at the University of Missouri in Columbia, and Angela Ginorio, a psychologist at Bowling Green State University, give regular and explicit attention to ethics in all of their teaching. In his course on criminology, for example, Galliher questions the ethics of the theoretical paradigms used in studying deviance and crime and of government-sponsored research whose net effect is to control the lives of the poor. Similarly, Ginorio spends at least one session on the ethics of research and theory-construction in her courses on Human Sexuality, the Psychology of Women, and Cross-Cultural Psychology. Michael Useem, a sociologist at Boston University, devotes one class meeting, and sometimes two, to the ethical, legal, and political aspects of social research in both his undergraduate and graduate courses on research methods.

Myron Glazer of Smith College not only teaches an entire course on ethics, but considers research ethics a focal point in two other courses.

> . . . each semester I teach an *introductory course* which focuses on a series of case studies so that students may have a clear sense of the precise work which sociologists do. . . this course stresses the sociological imagination and the interplay of conceptual thinking and empirical research. At the beginning of the course students read my book, *The Research Adventure*, and are immediately exposed to the significance of ethical and political issues in the sociological enterprise. As we analyze each case study, students are asked to think about the impetus for (the) research, the connections to other work done in the social sciences, and a decision as to the methodology and the ethical issues which the researchers had to confront.
>
> I have also recently introduced a course dealing with *Qualitative Methods in Social Research*. That course requires students to conduct an independent research project on some aspect of social movements or subcultures. Integral to that course is an emphasis on research methodology. Students read general statements in the area, as well as specific case material. In addition, . . . several researchers are invited to come to class and to present their studies. Their presentation focuses on substantive, methodological and ethical issues. In the Fall of 1977, we videotaped all of these researchers and used these tapes in the Fall 1978 course. Thus in several instances students viewed the tapes, and heard the same researchers speak about their projects a year later. The combination of tapes followed by an in-person visit is an excellent one.

Glazer's approach is to "teach ethics within a framework emphasizing the actual case studies from which the issues arise. That combination highlights the substantive, ethical, and personal components of any research project." Glazer has gone further than most in situating discussions of research ethics within the total context of a given project. His use of videotapes to bring home the ethical as well as the other dimensions of the research experience also seems unique.

William D'Antonio of the Sociology Department at the University of Connecticut makes a particular effort to raise ethical issues in his courses on introductory sociology. Building on the course text, which gives some attention to ethics, D'Antonio tries to extend the discussion at several points in the course. As he notes,

> For the most part the undergraduate students seem totally unprepared to think about such questions. Early on I try to sensitize them to the ideological and ethical implications of all social research. I also try to make them aware of the

ethical and ideological implications of materials brought into the classroom, and of the kinds of questions which the instructor may ask. Such discussions take place several times during a semester.

Ted Vaughan, a sociologist at the University of Missouri in Columbia, also regularly includes ". . . focused discussion on ethical issues as they relate to general sociological theory and theory construction." Andrew Weigert of the Department of Sociology and Anthropology at the University of Notre Dame takes an even broader view of the teaching of ethics. Rather than isolating this subject for separate treatment, he prefers to raise ethical issues, " . . . when my teaching touches on the boundary between sociology and ethics."

Finally, some social scientists conduct sessions on ethics as part of courses offered in professional schools. In his seminar on Socio-Legal Research at the University of Michigan Law School, Angus Campbell devotes one class to a comparison of ethical problems in the law and in the social sciences. As the former director of the Survey Research Center and the Institute for Social Research at Michigan, Campbell can draw on a wealth of research experience in his commentaries on ethics. Charles Lidz, a sociologist on the faculty of psychiatry at the University of Pittsburgh, lectures on the ethics of informed consent in that setting. From all indications many other social scientists now raise ethical issues in passing while teaching on almost any subject. Although they form but a small percentage of social scientists in the United States, their numbers have increased substantially over the last decade, and especially during the past five years.

C. Informal Discussions

Teaching in the social sciences is almost always defined to include the informal, unscheduled, and often uncredited contacts between faculty and students. In some cases, such as advising on doctoral dissertations, these contacts form part of the faculty member's "teaching load." In others, such as the discussions held during office hours, over lunch, on a research project, or in after-hours "bull sessions," the instructor submits no chits for credits, but most recognize the pedagogic value of these interactions. Indeed, small, liberal-arts colleges commonly stress such opportunities as integral to their brand of education. It would be a mistake, then, to exclude informal discussions of ethics from the purview of teaching.

While detailed information on this question is scant, all signs suggest heightened attention to ethics at the informal level. Sometimes the discussions take place within the semistructured atmosphere of academic advising and the approval of dissertations. Given the ubiquity of institutional review boards and mounting sensitivity to the potential embarrassments arising from ethical abuses, academic advisors are much more inclined now than a decade ago to question the ethics of student research. Critics of human subjects regulations charge, in fact, that graduate students are made to run such a long gauntlet of clearances that they are being discouraged from doing truly original field research. This charge will be explored later. The point here is that for reasons related as much to personal and institutional self-defense as to a positive concern with ethics, advisors are now raising ethical questions about deception, confidentiality, harm to subjects, and other aspects of social scientific research by students.

Similar discussions take place within research projects that may or may not involve academic credit. William Gamson, a social psychologist at the University of Michigan, found himself confronting major questions of ethics in a study built around an experimental hoax:

> For the last four years, I have been engaged in research that involves an elaborate fabrication. It inevitably raises serious ethical issues and we held a series of discussions of people working on the project—half a dozen graduate students and myself—reviewing literature on informed consent and on experimental hoaxing.

Gamson and his associates not only scrutinized the ethics of the research procedures before undertaking the fabrication, but carefully monitored the reactions of participants as the experiment moved along. Largely because of an ethical judgment that the level of stress was too high for certain individuals, they decided to end the project without completing the original design. By almost any theory of pedagogy, student exposure to ethical reflection in this setting would have to be rated as potent, with or without formal credit.

Several social scientists mentioned ethical discussions with students in even less structured circumstances, such as office hours. Among these were Peter Berger, Richard Adams, Ted Vaughan, Joan Sieber, Murray Wax, and Herbert Kelman. In my own case I have found many students at Harvard University concerned with ethics and seeking a forum for discussion, but often unsure about how even to broach the subject. Over the past year I have had several informal contacts with students on questions of ethics. Two undergraduate students, one from a course and the other not, have asked me to recommend them for summer internships at The Hastings Center. Both were intensely interested in questions of ethics and saw the internship as an ideal way to pursue these interests without a major commitment of time and money. I have also served on the dissertation committee of a doctoral student studying the ethics of international population programs.

D. Tributary Activities

Even more striking than the upswing in the teaching of ethics within academic settings has been the recent spurt in conferences, seminars, projects, sessions at professional meetings, and writings on ethics in the social sciences. Should some or all of these para-academic activities be considered forms of teaching? The answer depends on how we define teaching. For example, one common form of graduate instruction takes place when a student, with minimal supervision, sets out to read a given block of literature. By a very broad definition of teaching, those who contribute to this literature are engaged in the teaching enterprise. Sessions conducted at the annual meetings of professional associations in anthropology, sociology, or psychology would meet a less sweeping criterion of teaching. After all, we do encourage our students, especially our graduate students, to attend annual meetings, in good part to familiarize themselves with the current issues and cast of characters in their chosen discipline. To head off needless quibbling about definitions, perhaps the most sensible approach is to regard these activities as tributaries flowing into mainstream teaching in the social sciences. Some undertakings, such as conferences held in university settings and involving significant numbers of students, would be at the nexus of tributary and river, while others, such as writing projects undertaken by nonacademic soloists, would be further removed from the main current. Whatever the case, the activities in question have undoubtedly facilitated and probably stimulated more structured forms of teaching.

The period between 1977 and 1979 was marked by a sharp rise in the number of conferences and allied meetings on ethics in the social sciences. Particularly notable was the number of meetings concerned with ethical problems in anthropological fieldwork. Two of the leaders in recent discussions about fieldwork have been Murray Wax, an anthropologist at Washington University, and Joan Cassell, an anthropologist with the Center for Policy Research in New York. Wax is principal investigator and Cassell the executive director of a project on "Ethical Problems in Fieldwork" funded by the National Science Foundation. The following statement on the project's goals reflects a strong concern with pedagogy in the broadest sense:

> The task of the investigators is to begin the definition and analysis of the ethical issues of fieldwork, to sensitize experienced fieldworkers and graduate students to these issues, and to encourage professional associations to establish procedures for self-regulation.

In relation to this project, Wax and Cassell have conducted sessions on ethics at the annual meetings of the American Association for the Advancement of Science in 1977 and the American Anthropological Association in 1977 and 1978. They also organized a workshop based on case histories of fieldwork at the annual meeting of the Society for Applied Anthropology in the spring of 1979. Their session at the AAAS led to the publication of a book on ethics.[12]

A somewhat different focus was seen in the Conference on Solutions to Ethical and Legal Dilemmas in Social Research, held in February, 1978. Organized by Robert Boruch, Joseph Cecil, and Jerry Ross of the Psychology Department of Northwestern University, the conference sought concrete solutions to such problems as informed consent, scapegoating or labeling resulting from social research, invasions of privacy, and violations of confidentiality. The emphasis of the conference was on technical, procedural, and statistical solutions rather than on the ethics of research in itself. Papers were presented on a variety of topics, including statistical, statutory, and procedural solutions to problems of privacy and confidentiality; the empirical bases for understanding consent in randomized experiments; problems of government clearance; and the role of institutional review boards.

In the fall of 1978, The Hastings Center held a conference on ethical issues in survey research, including commercial market research and public opinion polls. The meeting, which involved experts from commercial as well as university-based survey organizations, explored issues ranging from the ethics of research design (sampling, questionnaire construction, analysis, etc.) to the need for federal regulation of surveys and polls. The Kennedy Center for Bioethics at Georgetown University held a broadly focused conference on ethical issues in social science research in September, 1979. The issues addressed included harm and benefit, privacy and confidentiality, informed consent and deception, and government regulations. These and similar meetings contribute directly to the formal teaching of ethics by providing papers and other materials which can be incorporated into classroom discussions. They also contribute indirectly by encouraging and legitimizing the discussion of ethical issues and by suggesting new questions and lines of ethical inquiry that might be pursued with students.

Also a vital contributor to the teaching of ethics is the expanding volume of written material available. Several textbooks and collections of readings have appeared since 1977, and others are in preparation. Articles on ethics also appear more frequently now than a decade ago in the leading professional journals. While the newsletter of the American Anthropological Association has long published articles on the ethics and politics of anthropological research, such writings have been less frequent in sociology and psychology journals. It was thus a significant departure when *The American Sociologist,* an official journal of the American Sociological Association, devoted almost its entire issue of August, 1978, to questions of research ethics. Another notable development is that veteran researchers who had never previously commented on the ethics of their work are beginning to do so. Although ethics has hardly taken any of these fields by storm, the subject now surfaces with a regularity that would have surprised this writer even five years ago.

If explicit teaching about ethics in the social sciences is of quite recent origin, the essential concern behind it is not. Responsible practitioners of anthropology, psychology, and sociology have long taught their students, as much by deed as by word, to respect those whom they study, to follow high standards of honesty in gathering and reporting data, to avoid compromising situations with research sponsors, and to refrain from behaviors which might damage the professions. I recently remarked to Angus Campbell, former head of the Survey Research Center at the University of Mighican, that while I rarely heard the word "ethics" during my time there, I was taught a strong sense of responsibility in practicing survey research. We learned that the honest survey researcher must draw a sample that is representative of the population about which generalizations are to be made, avoid bias in the design of questionnaires and interview schedules, ensure that bias is not introduced by the interviewing process, explore all relevant avenues in analysis, rather than only those which might please the sponsor, and report findings within the limits of the sampling and other errors inherent in the study. Campbell replied that social scientists "are teaching ethics to their younger associates every day although, like you, they are probably unaware that they are being taught." The teaching of ethics has clearly gone beyond the instruction in the craft noted by Campbell, but we should not forget that many social scientists have long tried to inculcate high ethical standards in their students even though they did not use that expression to describe their efforts. This is not to imply that there is nothing new in the teaching of ethics, but that some of what we now see being discussed openly went on in earlier years quietly and implicitly.

E. Goals in the Teaching of Ethics

When social scientists engage in the teaching of ethics, what do they hope to accomplish? Although very few respondents commented explicitly on the goals of their teaching in this field, their remarks suggest several broad and interwoven aspirations. (For general goals for teaching ethics, see *The Teaching of Ethics in Higher Education: A Report by The Hasting Center*.[13])

The first and most basic goal appears to be the *development of a sense of professional responsibility*. If pressed about why they include material on ethics in their courses, many social scientists would say that it is to make students aware of their obligations to the individuals studied, to the relevant professions, to one's own society, and, in the case of crossnational research, to other societies. A good number of those now teaching about ethics became interested in the subject as a result of personal concern about abuses in social scientific research. It is thus not surprising that they see the teaching of ethics as a way of preventing such abuses in the future. Some also feel a personal and professional obligation to help fledgling researchers avoid the embarrassment that often arises from the use of questionable research tactics, such as deception or the falsification of one's identity as a researcher. And more than a few consider it their obligation as teachers to instruct students in the practicalities of local and national ethical codes, including local rules covering the protection of human subjects.

A second goal is the *development of analytical skills* related to ethics. Perhaps the most fundamental is the sheer ability to recognize an ethical issue when it appears. Given the strongly positivistic orientation of the social sciences, especially sociology and psychology, one of the greatest barriers to discussing ethics is uncertainty about what the term implies and skepticism about whether it is relevant to the discipline in question. Many instructors consider it a sign of intellectual progress when students in the social sciences are able to identify an ethical issue and handle it as such, rather than immediately reduce it to another research question. For example, in debates over the acceptability of deception, there is still resistance to the idea of treating deception as a moral issue in its own right, rather than a set of empirical hypotheses about subject reactions to being deceived. Once students can recognize ethical issues, instructors are in a position to introduce concepts, principles, and other analytical tools for exploring their meaning. My sense is that very few courses reach the point of developing well-focused analytical skills. Most instructors, I suspect, consider themselves quite fortunate if their students come away from a course with an ability to sight and articulate ethical issues. Many do not themselves have especially good skills in ethical analysis, as distinct from issue-raising, and even among those who do, time is usually too short for detailed discussion of concepts and principles.

A third goal is the *stimulation of critical reflection* on the values embodied in, created by, and served through the social sciences. This aim is related to, but somewhat different from, the development of analytical skills. This last phrase implies an ability to recognize an ethical issue, such as the use of deception, and to handle it with the tools of moral philosophy and allied disciplines. The stimulation of critical reflection entails searching analysis of the values involved in all aspects of the discipline, from the assumptions made about individual behavior and social structure to the choice of concepts and methods for research to the uses made of the intellectual products of a given discipline. Thus, one instructor goes to some lengths in examining the moral and political values underlying the entire field of criminology. Others probe the dilemmas arising from the ubiquity of values in social research and the simultaneous demands for objectivity. While much of this analysis forms part of the philosophy of the social sciences, those aspects focusing specifically on ethical and moral values can be considered part of the teaching of ethics.

Individual instructors, of course, will have their own personal goals in teaching about ethics, and these will be as diverse as the people involved. Some may use critical reflection as a way of debunking the entire enterprise of social science, or of showing how it is a servant of capitalist or socialist ideologies. Others will be committed to the teaching of ethics because of a belief that the ethical researcher will also be the effective researcher in the field. Some contacted in this study were worried that ethical abuses would lead to a growing set of restrictions on research, and they were convinced that reciprocity with participants was not only good ethics but sound practice. As is always true with teaching, personal agendas and pedagogical goals may be quite different and yet still mutually supportive.

II. Personal Origins of Involvement

The teaching of ethics is still limited, but much more extensive now than even ten years ago. In 1959 the social scientists who taught explicitly about ethics were very few and their message was largely disregarded by their disciplines. By 1969 there were perhaps fifteen to twenty individuals who gave serious and manifest attention to ethical questions in their teaching. As of 1979 that number is at least one hundred, and if we include those who raise "questions of ethics" in passing, it would be considerably larger. Whatever the indicator, there is little doubt that ethics has acquired a visible, if small and often ambivalent, presence in all the social sciences.

What accounts for the change? The best explanation involves a combination of contextual and personal factors. Obviously a potent force for change was the strong public reaction against ethical abuses in research with human subjects, and the governmental regulations that followed. Faced with a labyrinth of rules and clearances impinging directly on their opportunities for research, many social scientists became interested in ethics as a matter of self-defense. But even before these regulations took hold there were a few who spoke out on ethical matters, and afterward some were more likely than others to gravitate in that direction. Hence, to understand the heightened interest in ethics, we must look both to the ethos of the social science disciplines and to the personal background of the social scientists. I will begin by reviewing the patterns of personal involvement with the teaching of ethics.

Several common elements appear in the background of those

presently involved in the teaching of ethics. One group seems to have been drawn to this field because of its resonance with their own long-standing interests in philosophy, theology, or simply morality. Herbert Kelman, for instance, traces his involvement with ethics directly to his training in Jewish theology. When he moved into graduate school in social psychology at Yale, he brought with him the deeply held conviction that man is an end rather than a means. His earliest concerns about the ethics of the social sciences grew out of situations that he felt might violate or undercut that principle, particularly those involving the manipulation of human behavior. Among the areas where manipulation seemed to raise ethical issues were sensitivity training (T-Groups), research on job satisfaction and morale in industry, and organized techniques of persuasion through communications. Although Kelman began to speak about these questions in the late 1940s and continued his interest through the 1950s, it was not until the 1960s that he began to write about ethics in the social sciences. He recalls that in the intervening years ethics was not a frequent topic of discussion or an area of explicit concern in these fields, so that there were few organized opportunities to present papers and otherwise become involved in writing. As the ethos began to change in the 1960s, particularly with the debates in social psychology over the ethics of deception, Kelman's involvement in this area increased substantially.

Another social scientist who has taught in this field attributes his current involvement to philosophical interests acquired during his undergraduate years:

I did my undergraduate work at the University of Chicago (where Jewish professors taught Thomistic doctrines to atheist students). For whatever reasons, the curriculum seemed to be infused with an interest in, and concern for, the moral and ethical implications of knowledge. This has remained with me. The major reason, I believe, was that the Chicago faculty were agreed upon a sophisticated image of the educated person and this included, willy-nilly, a moral dimension.

He adds: ". . . I am waiting and wanting to see a revival of the general, lively interest in moral and ethical questions which (I fancy) existed in my student days." Several others traced their concern with ethics to a religious background, training in the

Jesuit order, or academic studies in philosophy. One prominent sociologist simply said: "I am, and always have been, a *moraliste*."

For others the catalyst of ethical concern was direct experience with value dilemmas in the conduct of their own research. The precipitating studies included research on draft resisters and student protest in the charged political atmosphere of the 1960s, small group experiments involving deception, field research on American Indians and other groups, and political research in Chile. A social psychologist commented: "I became interested when I began, for the first time, to do research which involved deception and was forced to come to terms with difficult ethical questions in my own work." A sociologist related this experience:

> My interest in the teaching of ethics stems from my doctoral research conducted in Chile in 1963–64 . . . that research especially alerted me to the personal, ethical, and political challenges of conducting research in a new environment. Those issues arise with particular potency when the effort is made to study a highly charged political situation.

For one renowned field researcher the pull toward ethical consciousness arose from a concern for reciprocity with those he studied:

> My own research has always depended heavily upon the cooperation of members of organizations or communities I study. I have always been concerned about how I could repay individuals and organizations in communities for the help I receive and especially with my obligation to avoid doing harm to individuals, organizations, or communities.

A third group became interested in ethics largely out of a reaction against ethical abuses in work by others. Most often cited as galvanizers of concern were the experiments on obedience conducted by Stanley Milgram; Project Camelot, an abortive study on social change, conflict, and "insurgency" in the developing countries; and *Tearoom Trade*, an investigation of male homosexuality in public restrooms.[14] A veteran sociologist describes his own evolution toward ethical awareness in these terms:

> As I have thought about the questions (in the questionnaire), I came to realize that I have indeed undergone considerable change in my orientation toward

ethical problems in recent years. More than anything else, I think it is fair to say I never used to think about them. I guess I assumed that what I did was probably ethical or I wouldn't be doing it. Looking back, I see that some aspects of participant observation were probably questionable, as were uses of scales which presumably measured one's degree of open or closed-mindedness.

Camelot and Tearoom Trade both caused me to begin some serious thought on the subject. I had been asked if I would be interested in participating in Camelot. The little information I was given suggested an exciting project which might yield some new models for significant social reform . . . but since Vietnam and the revelations about the CIA I have come to doubt the propriety of such research.

Another sociologist traced his ethical interests to the approaches used in an entire field of inquiry, rather than in any single study. He writes: "I became convinced that social scientists studying deviance and crime unthinkingly went about the business of invading the lives of the poor to help the government control these people." A psychologist remarked that her interest in the teaching of ethics developed "when I realized that science is not value-free; when I saw the (mis)use of science applied to minority populations."

Respondents also identified several other sources of interest in ethics. Two anthropologists mentioned their concern with the mounting governmental regulation of social research, and their feeling that the regulatory model used was inappropriate to their discipline. Several individuals indicated that teaching in areas allied to ethics, such as the dynamics of the research process, moved them toward a more explicit concern with the teaching of ethics. Others mentioned the stimulation provided by conversations with mentors involved in ethics or through contacts with The Hastings Center.

My own interest springs from a combination of the factors mentioned. Certainly the most powerful influence was an undergraduate background in philosophy and theology, and subsequent graduate training (and, briefly, teaching) in philosophy. When I entered the highly positivistic psychology department at the University of Michigan, I experienced a sharp clash between my concern for normative issues and the reigning empiricism of that setting. But since ethics was unmentioned, and in some spheres unmentionable, I pursued my philosophical interests through private reading and conversations with friends. When I began to teach at Oberlin College in 1963, I explored questions of values and the social sciences with students in Introductory Sociology, but did not move very far into ethics. It was only when I came to Harvard in 1967 and taught a course on comparative international research that I began to deal explicitly with the ethics of the social sciences. One specific source of stimulation was Project Camelot, which had cast a pall over international studies and virtually forced those of us teaching about international research to address the moral and political issues at stake. When Herbert Kelman came to Harvard in 1968, we decided to offer a course together on the politics and ethics of social research. From that point on, ethics became a significant element in my own identity as a social scientist.

III. Disciplinary Climates: Past and Present

If personal background plays a critical role in predisposing individuals toward or away from ethics, the climates in the social science disciplines are an even more potent influence on teaching in this field. Without a supportive environment an interest in ethics will usually not emerge at all, and when it does appear it will languish without nurturance from significant others. Of course, the distinction between person and environment should not be overdrawn, for persons make up a large part of the professional environment, and their actions can and do change its character. Nevertheless, the intellectual interests of social scientists, as of all professional specialists, are highly elastic to the collective fads, fashions, expectations, role models, and reward structures of their disciplines. It was not accidental that when the natural science model formed the prototype for sociology and psychology, overt concern with ethics was virtually nil, or that when this model began to crack, ethical concern once again came forward. It will be helpful, therefore, to have a brief overview of the place of ethics in social sciences from their emergence as separate disciplines to the present. Owing to my limited competence in the history of anthropology, the following discussions will deal mainly with sociology and psychology.

A. Early History

As is ritualistically pointed out in introductory courses, the present-day social sciences all trace their origins to philosophy. Well into the twentieth century, sociology and anthropology were closely tied to moral philosophy and were the subject of many attempts to create a new "moral science." It would be only a slight exaggeration to say that their founders saw these fields as vehicles for teaching a new, science-based morality. Contemporary concerns about the ethics of the discipline, such as the protection of human subjects in sociological research, would have been foreign to August Comte, Herbert Spencer, William Graham Sumner, Lester Ward, Albion Small, E.B. Tylor, and other pioneers of sociology and anthropology. Though in different ways and with different emphases, these thinkers all had a broad vision of social progress through an improved understanding of human society; in tone and in substance their writings were much closer to political theorists and moral philosophers than to the current harvest of publications on ethics and the social sciences. Their central concern was with the total society rather than the "human subject," with the macrodynamics of the social order rather than the microdynamics of social research.

The central place of morality, it not of ethics, was most evident with August Comte, one of the several reputed fathers of sociology. Comte's belief in scientific objectivity and its benefits for the welfare of humanity was almost a caricature of the humanistic positivism of American social science in the 1950s. The difference was that Comte had the nerve to proclaim openly what his successors consigned to occasional delusions. As an unabashed evolutionist, Comte saw societies moving inexorably from fetishism to monotheism to Western revolution, such as that seen in France, to the highest stage of positivism. Enter sociology at this highest stage to gather a store of positive knowledge for promoting social reconstruction and benevolence for all. The basis of the resulting society was to be a new morality inculcated through a positive educational system. In this reconstructed order the sociologists would form a new priesthood, replacing the theologians of an earlier era. They would be the scientific directors, interpreting the doctrines of positivism, and also the managers of the educational system. No one before or after, with the exception of B.F. Skinner, has accorded social scientists such political and ethical distinction. If today Comte is widely dismissed as a dreamer and is treated as an embarrassment in courses on sociological theory, he can certainly not be criticized for inattention to ethics.

The pioneers of sociology in the United States, such as Albion Small, were much less ambitious in their political and moral aspirations for the social sciences. Small was the founder of the Sociology Department at the University of Chicago, a department with a pervasive impact on the shape of American sociology. Like Comte, Small saw sociology as a unifying science drawing together all fields of knowledge bearing on man and society, including moral philosophy. His touchstone for assaying knowledge was not such notions as the reliability and validity of data, but the extent to which it showed mankind what was worth doing. He and many of his contemporaries hoped that scientific studies of society would provide the basis for concrete moral guidance and, ideally, a universal ethic for humanity. But even during his own administration of the department, his Chicago colleagues, with his tacit cooperation, gradually clipped the wings of such ambitions and stayed closer to the ground of empirical observation.

The history of the Chicago department recapitulates the progressive dilution of explicit moral concern in the entire discipline of sociology. Small was succeeded by a generation of scholars, such as Robert Park, Louis Wirth, and Ernest Burgess, who were not lacking in moral passion, but who wanted sociology to be more of a science. The studies of the "Chicago School" on social disorganization began with a strong sense of concern for those thought to be suffering the ravages of urbanization, migration, and other kinds of social change. But their authors generally kept their personal values in the background, allowing them to shape the choice of topics, the approach to research, and the tone of presentation, but not to come forward in full dress. And it was not long before a reaction set in against would-be preachers, reformers, and do-gooders in the social sciences. Even in the 1920s, the view was spreading that sociology should discover new knowledge through systematic observation and other methodologies while eschewing any overt reformist ambitions. By 1930 there was a widely shared conviction, at Chicago and elsewhere, that sociology should be a scientific discipline with its own theories, methods, and professional identity. The high priesthood envisioned by Comte was safely interred in the archives of sociological history, to be resurrected for inspection, but never for imitation. The flowing robes of the priest had been replaced by the business suit of the professor.

Because psychology's primordial ties to moral philosophy were more tenuous than those of sociology or anthropology, its separation from explicit ethical concerns was correspondingly easier. The branch of philosophy from which the present disciplines emerged was what is now called the philosphy of man, a tradition less involved in ethical deliberations. While such questions as the nature of man, the structure of the mind, the role of emotions, and the dominant human motives involved ethical assumptions and implications, the precursors of modern psychology were not as wedded to moral philosophy as their counterparts in sociology. The person most commonly identified as the father of psychology is Wilhelm Wundt, who opened the first psychological laboratory in 1879. Although Wundt's own interests spanned psychology, ethics, culture, and linguistics, his successors selected, reinterpreted, and exalted those elements of his work most suited to the emerging behaviorism. And neither Wundt nor the new experimentalists had any articulated plan for social reconstruction or for installing psychologists as the architects of human destiny. Such Comtean ambitions would come much later in the writings of B. F. Skinner, and even then be regarded as an inspirational anomaly. Hence, despite Wundt's own breadth in philosophy, the transition from philosophy to scientific psychology was swift. A few writers, most notably William James, remained both philosophers and psychologists, but they were generally considered outside the mainstream of the discipline, at least in their philosophical interests. By 1930 the behaviorist views put forward by John B. Watson and others formed the dominant theoretical perspective of American psychology, and continue to this day. Behaviorism, explicitly and adamantly, has not had room for ethics or any kindred form of "philosophical speculation," for it purports to rest entirely on observation, experimentation, and other elements of the scientific method.

B. The Triumph of Positivism: 1930–65

From the 1930s through the 1950s the positivist mode of thought became ever more deeply entrenched in the disciplines of sociology and psychology. A philosophical force lending powerful support to tendencies already present was the logical positivism first developed by the Vienna Circle. As members of this school began to take positions in American universities in the 1930s, they found many enthusiastic adherents, not only in philosophy departments, but in the social sciences. The impact was enormous, even among many social scientists who had never heard of the Vienna School. Robert Friedrichs observes: ". . . the exodus from the Continent of the Circle members before the threat of Nazism and the re-establishment of key members in chairs of philosophy of science in leading American graduate schools largely guaranteed the predominance of logical positivism in the philosophical thinking of natural and social scientists in America during the 'forties and 'fifties."[15]

The essential tenet of logical positivism is that the truth of statements of fact must be established by observation; statements not based on observable data are meaningless. This principle bears directly on the scope for ethics in the social sciences and elsewhere. To have any meaning, ethical statements must either fall within the compass of observations ("students who are deceived by experiments will be hostile to social research") or otherwise be derived from science, as from an empirically based theory. In the earliest versions of positivism propagated by the Vienna Circle, the philosopher was portrayed almost as a criminal. This view carried over to the social sciences as well. When I took a course on psychometrics in the Psychology Department at Michigan, one of the readings was an essay by Rudolph Carnap on "The Methodological Character of Theoretical Concepts." In my comments on that particular reading, I disagreed with Carnap's assertion that "the usual questions of ontology are pseudo-questions without cognitive content." I stated that "there are things beyond the observable that constitute real problems in philosophy," including ethics. The instructor replied in the margin: "There *may* be for philosophy, but it is this viewpoint that Feigl has reference to when he says: 'Philosophy is the disease for which it ought to be the cure' and I agree." This individual was distinctive mainly in knowing the intellectual origins of his positivism. Many others in that department accepted its precepts with little notion of where they came from.

What positivism meant concretely for teaching was a paramount emphasis on the meaning, necessity, and value of the scientific method. Introductory textbooks in these fields, and the courses in which they were used, routinely began with discussions on the key requirements for a science and on how the discipline in question does, or should, meet those standards. One of the most popular textbooks in introductory psychology, for example, was that written by Clifford Morgan (later with Richard King). The following passages, taken from the 1966 edition, could be found in almost any major text, then or now:

> Psychology as a science is, first of all, *empirical*. That is to say, it rests on experiment and observation, rather than on argument, opinion, or belief . . .
>
> Another distinguishing feature of science is *measurement*. Almost all of us take it for granted that each science measures things . . .
>
> Careful *definition* of terms is essential to clear thinking in science . . .
>
> One way of making sure that we are defining concepts in terms of observables is to use operational definitions (Bridgman, 1927). When we define a concept operationally, we define it in terms of measurable and observable operations.[16]

Philosophy is discussed in the book only to show that science outgrew it; the term ethics does not appear at all. Similar definitions appear in the great majority of sociology texts. For example, a run-of-the-mill work by Sutherland, Woodward, and Maxwell defines sociology as a discipline relying on the scientific approach. This consists of certain assumptions and a method:

> The chief assumption is the belief that phenomena occur in an orderly and natural fashion.
>
> The method consists of observation (using one or more of the five senses) and verification—both carried on in as systematic and controlled a fashion as possible.[17]

While the book does have a few pages on "mores," it makes no mention of ethics, morality, or of philosophy more generally. This pattern was very typical of most introductory works on psychology and sociology published in the 1950s and 1960s. The message to hundreds of thousands of introductory students was clear: the social sciences are *really* scientific, and have no place for soft speculation about ethics.

If the scientific method was the road to perfection, value neutrality was the required garb for travel. The moral equation was simple: science = objectivity; objectivity = value neutrality; *ergo*, science = value neutrality. It was Max Weber who first clearly articulated the need for separating facts from values in the scientific sphere, and who advocated value neutrality for the scientist *qua* scientist.[18] In fact, Weber did not go to the extremes often ascribed to him in simplistic summaries of his views, but he did legitimize the dualism between facts and values. Less sophisticated American social scientists pushed the principle of neutrality, and the consequent exclusion of ethics, to absurd extremes. In a book entitled *Can Science Save Us,* the sociologist George Lundberg argued that value-free sociology cannot afford the "luxury of indignation," "personalistic and moralistic inter- pretations," or "deeply cherished ideologies resembling in form if not in content their theological predecessor." The last phrase was particularly interesting given the title of the book. Robert Friedrichs offers these reflections on Lundberg's latent ethics:

> . . . his identification of objectivity with ethical neutrality was unusual only because he spoke to and for the position a decade or two earlier than most of his contemporaries. But it was integral to the image of the sociologist projected by that instrument of professional socialization—the introductory text—almost without exception over the past two decades following World War II. Students entering the field during that period had every reason to accept the command- ment that sociologists should say nothing about the "goodness" or "evil" of human social behavior. Their task, like the natural scientists', was to discover empirical uniformities that could be used to predict and control other empirical phenomena. Woe to the doctoral candidate who dared question the union of objectivity with neutrality.[19]

Despite the pleas for neutrality from Lundberg and others, the value problem simply would not go away. Try as they might, the strict positivists could not unearth an epistemology that would free knowledge from the taint of subjectivity. The next attempt to grapple with the problem was truly ingenious, for it would have us derive normative judgments from empirical observations. Rather than trying to separate the inseparable, the trick was to place the two in the same paradigm, with hard facts serving as legitimation for soft values. With his usual bravado Lundberg abruptly did away with the need for ethics:

> I am prepared to argue that the whole preoccupation of mankind throughout the centuries with the word "ought" has been merely another semantic confusion. Such a statement as "we ought not to steal" *and any other "ought" statement whatsoever,* can be shown to owe its peculiarity and its apparent difference from any other ordinary scientific statement of fact to certain unspoken premises which are always implied in "ought" statments. Actually it amounts to this: If we steal, then we are likely to suffer retribution; then don't steal. When "ought" statements are thus fully stated they become identical with other scientific statements, all of which are of the "if . . then" type. That is, *they are predictions of what will probably occur under stated conditions,* and in this respect differ not at all from scientific statements except that the probability and conditions of the former have not as yet been so fully worked out.[20]

While intellectually appealing to the devout positivist, Lundberg's prescription implied much more work than most social scientists were prepared to give the quest for values. Rather than laboriously dredging up moral principles from murky and usually incomplete data, most dealt with the value dilemma in other ways.

For some, the simplest course was to take one's ethics from religion, political ideology, or prevailing norms in the larger society. Commenting on the questions raised for this study, the social psychologist Daniel Katz remarks:

> There has been little general recognition of the need for consideration of ethical problems as such. This is due in good part, I believe, to the fact that existing social values and the constraints employed by pressure groups are substitutes for social science ethics. In other words, we take over the values of the society instead of developing an ethics of our own. In part this is due to the fact that these value systems existed as relevant to a given set of problems long before they were investigated by social scientists. For example, the values of management were a dominant force before industrial psychology and helped to influence it. And the taboos about sex affected the development of knowledge in that area. In other words, social scientists were slow to develop an ethics of their own because the problems they dealt with were so close to existing social values.

A second way of coping with the tensions between science and values was compartmentalization. Many prominent social scientists in the 1940s and the 1950s were individuals of strong moral and political commitments. Some had been personally exposed to fascism or kindred forms of totalitarianism, while others had been singed by McCarthyism. Colleagues who studied sociology at Columbia University specifically cite Robert Lynd, Paul Lazersfeld, and C. Wright Mills as scholars with strong and explicit value commitments. Some of these were able to translate their moral concerns into social scientific research, as with studies on the authoritarian personality, on the class structure of the United States, or on political conformity. Others, most notably Mills, adopted an openly critical posture that shunned the trappings of positivism and the pretense of value freedom. But for many it was difficult to build solid bridges between personal commitments and professional research, so that the only viable solution was to segregate the roles of person and professional, citizen and scientist. Thus Paul Lazersfeld, who was known to his students as much for the strength of his value commitments as for the sophistication of his methodology, influenced the discipline of sociology mostly as a researcher and methodologist. And it is significant that among the next generation of sociologists trained at Columbia there are relatively few known today for their explicit attempts to bring together moral commitments and scientific research. Perhaps sensing the difficulties faced by their mentors in reconciling commitment with objectivity, social scientists trained in the 1940s and 1950s seemed to take compartmentalization even further.

A third form of reconciliation, often combined with one of the previous, was to attribute strong moral value to the scientific enterprise itself. A syllogism which I encountered in implicit form many times during graduate school went as follows: social science is science; science contributes to human welfare; therefore social science contributes to human welfare. Thus, the animal psychologist whose life work was to study conditioning on the left hind leg of the white rat could take consolation from the contributions of such research to human betterment. Even those who were vehemently opposed to value judgments in social science, and considered philosophy a blight on the intellectual landscape, could embrace ethics at this level.

Finally, there were many who simply screened out any concern with ethics and got on with the business of social science.

Confronted with the value dilemma that so vexed George
Lundberg, they shrugged and said it didn't matter. By the 1950s
the passion of a Lundberg had typically been replaced by the
coolness of the practicing researcher who had neither the time nor
the inclination to take on the larger problems of ethics and
values. Value questions might surface from time to time in one's
scientific work, but they should best be ignored or left to others
with more of a taste for the subject.

C. The Return of Ethics: 1965–79

Beginning around 1965, and with mounting frequency over the
next five years, the word "ethics" began to be heard in all of the
social sciences. This time it was not in the context of Comtean
chimeras or Lundbergian antinomies, but in the spirit of protest.
The leitmotiv of most discussions was ethical *abuses*. Liberals
were concerned about deceptions, invasions of privacy, and other
harm to human subjects. Radicals charged that entire disciplines
were a form of abuse, serving the interests of American imperial-
ism, exploiting the domestic poor in the interests of the powerful,
and working to reinforce an exploitative status quo at home and
abroad. Given the particular thrust of ethics as it reemerged in
this period, and current responses to this genealogy, it will be
helpful to review the major precipitators of ethical concern.

Before considering these factors, it is important to note that the
triumph of positivism in psychology and sociology was never
complete. As with the Aztec conquests in Mexico, there were
always pockets of outright resistance and veins of opposition that
could be exploited with a shift in political circumstances. In
sociology there were numerous scholars who had never embraced
the positivist ethic and its stance of value neutrality. Among
these were Robert Bierstedt, Kurt Wolff, Peter Berger, Robert
Nisbet, Lewis Coser, C. Wright Mills, Arthur Vidich, Alfred
McClung Lee, Howard Becker, John Seeley, and Gideon
Sjoberg. In the 1960s several of these individuals took issue with
the professions' putative ethical neutrality and called for greater
attention to morality and human values. In 1962 Alvin Gouldner
published an influential essay entitled "Anti-Minotaur: The Myth

of Value-Free Sociology." Gouldner argued that Weber's oft-cited proclamation on value neutrality had to be understood in the specific context of German universities in his time and that Weber had never intended to banish values from sociology. In psychology the counterforces against positivism were smaller, but still significant. What has now become the movement for humanistic psychology had its precursors in the 1950s, including Carl Rogers and Abraham Maslow. The Society for the Psychological Study of Social Issues, which included many prominent social psychologists, was consciously and explicitly concerned with values, if not ethics as such. But in the early 1960s there was less ethical ferment in psychology than in sociology. Psychologists on the whole seemed less inclined to question their discipline's basic moral paradigms, and more willing to live with compartmentalization between personal and professional roles.

The most powerful blow against ethical neutrality and its positivist roots came from the student movement of the 1960s. Some of the founding members of the New Left came from the social sciences and were not slow to apply their critical tools to the disciplines closest at hand. Thus at the meetings of the American Sociological Association in 1968, Martin Nicolaus, representing the Sociology Liberation Movement, delivered his now-famous remarks to the convention. Charging that sociology is an outgrowth of nineteenth-century European conservatism and wedded to twentieth-century corporate liberalism, he lambasted almost every aspect of sociological theory and practice:

> Sociology is not now and never has been any kind of objective seeking out of social truth or reality . . .
>
> Sociologists stand guard in the garrison and report to its masters on the movement of the occupied populace. The more adventurous sociologists don the disguise of the people and go out to mix with the peasants in the "field," returning with books and articles that break the protective secrecy in which a subjected population wraps itself, and make it more accessible to manipulation and control.[21]

Though Nicolaus would have disdained the term "ethics" as bourgeois rhetoric, his assault on value neutrality was direct, vehement, widely heard, and couched in unequivocally moral terms.

At about the same time, radical members of the American Anthropological Association began to publish commentaries, which continue to the present, on the theme of "Anthropology as Colonialism." These radical critiques soon found their way into the cloisters of academe, sometimes quietly, sometimes obstreperously. One specific outcropping was a course offered in Harvard's Department of Social Relations in 1968–69. Ostensibly taught by faculty and concerned with social change, it was, in fact, largely conducted by students and served as a vehicle for social criticism on many fronts. These critiques originating from the New Left rarely advocated explicit attention to ethics, but by rending the cloak of neutrality and highlighting the power dimensions of the social sciences they set the stage for work by others. This association between radicalism and ethics in the social sciences has not been forgotten by those who lived through the sixties, and affects current perceptions of the teaching of ethics.

One event that did draw specific attention to the ethics of social scientific research was the ill-starred Project Camelot. If the student movement undermined the assumption of objectivity in the social sciences, Camelot called into question the widely held notion that American social scientists could freely roam the world in the pursuit of truth. Project Camelot was a multi-million dollar effort launched by the United States Army to develop new approaches to the prediction and control of social change, political conflict, and military "insurgency" in the developing countries. It was aborted during its planning stages in 1965, but not before it had touched off a furor in Latin America and elsewhere, including Washington. In the wake of Camelot, many social scientists, particularly sociologists, anthropologists, and political scientists, became explicitly aware of both the political and ethical pitfalls involved in crosscultural research. Dozens of articles and at least two books appeared on this subject in the United States, and the debate rapidly spread throughout Latin America and other developing countries.[22] Even today, the ghost of Camelot rises up, like an evil genie, from murky cases of international research.

Also fanning the flames of ethical concern was the war in Vietnam. While growing American involvment in Indochina lent impetus to the critiques expressed by the New Left, it also aroused pervasive misgivings among those not inclined to radical-

ism. Many veteran social scientists began to question the acceptance of funds from such sources as the Advanced Research
Projects Agency of the Army or other branches of the military.
Even stronger criticisms were directed against social scientists
who actively cooperated with the military, or gave the appearance
of doing so. In a widely read article entitled "Anthropology on
the Warpath," two anthropologists questioned the morality of
data-gathering for the military in Indochina. *Human Organization,* the journal of the Society for Applied Anthropology, began
to devote increasing space to the ethics of field research, not only
in Vietnam or Laos, but with minority populations in the United
States. This link between political concern and the ethics of
research in anthropology has created the lingering perception that
the teaching of ethics in that field is an offshoot of politics.

On the domestic scene, several related developments sparked
explicit interest in the ethics of social research. One was the
mounting public outcry against invasions of privacy by government, business, and other institutions. If the central focus of this
protest was the computer, social scientific research, which was
often intrusive in nature and generated highly sensitive data for
storage in computers, also came up for scrutiny. Within the
social sciences themselves there was a growing reaction against
alleged abuses of human subjects. Beginning about 1965, several
writers, led by Herbert Kelman, questioned the ethics of deception in social research and the treatment of subjects in studies
such as the obedience experiments conducted by Stanley Milgram. Toward the end of the 1960s the campaign for subject
protection moved into high gear, with support from legislators as
well as concerned individuals in the professions. The founding of
The Hastings Center in 1969 both symbolized and reinforced the
emerging consensus about the salience of ethics, including the
ethics of the social sciences. Several social scientists, including
myself, have been associated with the Center from its very
beginning, and it has consistently addressed ethical issues arising
in and around the social sciences. More recently, stringent government regulations on the protection of human subjects have
created an atmosphere in which even the most hard-bitten advocates of the scientific method are confronted willy-nilly with the
empirical consequences of ethical concern.

Taken together this confluence of forces has created an environment in which writing and teaching about ethics is at least minimally respectable, if not actively rewarded. Had Herbert Kelman and I tried in 1959 to offer a seminar on the politics and ethics of social research, the basic concept would have been little understood and the validity of such a course actively challenged. By 1969 the rationale was much more intelligible, and the idea on its face not outrageous. Teaching about ethics has made the leap from oblivion to ambivalence, where it now rests.

IV. Present Attitudes Toward Teaching

Now that ethics is a fairly frequent topic of discussion in social science departments, how is it regarded by faculty, students, and administrators? To get at this question my survey asked several questions about the present atmosphere for teaching. One of the most useful was:

How would you characterize the attitudes of your professional colleagues toward the teaching of ethics? Are they enthusiastic, mildly supportive, tolerant or indifferent, wary or hostile. Cite any specifics illustrating or supporting your judgment.

The replies, which were sometimes lengthy and detailed, suggest a variety of departmental situations, but nonetheless a recognizable pattern of attitudes.

The most common reaction reported from professional colleagues might be termed wary indifference. Many said, in essence, that they were free to teach about ethics if they so chose, but that their efforts in this field sparked no enthusiasm and some suspicion within their departments. The following comments were typical:

Most of my colleagues regard discussion of ethics the way Victorians regarded discussion of sex; they don't understand what the discussion would involve and are sure that such a discussion would be harmful (to science). Most assume that a discussion of ethics would involve a discussion of who is an unethical person. They are not able to see that a critical evaluation of social science methodology might be useful to the social sciences (psychologist).

Most of my colleagues are relatively indifferent or wary, and few are sympathetic. They do not generally see any ethical dilemmas in the work they do although they would undoubtedly see more in the work of social psychologists who use deception (sociologist).

Indifferent and embarrassed in a nonspecific way (anthropologist).

Even one of the social scientists who has taught an entire course on ethics gave this reply to the question about colleagues' attitudes: "Wary, as am I."

These questionnaire responses, my own observations, and the literature in the field suggest several sources of wariness. Perhaps the most deeply rooted is the feeling that ethics and the scientific method are antagonistic. For some social scientists, ethics signifies either a return to the spongy speculations of yesteryear or a mass of conjectures that are unverified, arcane, and thus intellectually suspect. For others, the field evokes images of institutional review boards, government clearances, consent forms, and other operating obstacles to the progress of science. For still others, particularly social psychologists, it implies the ominous and ever-present threat of personal criticism for unethical behavior, departmental controversy over the proper limits of scientific investigation, or other forms of trouble. In the eyes of many, the teaching of ethics is but a subsidiary of the larger and bothersome enterprise of ethics.

Also at work is the widespread and partially justified perception that the teaching of ethics is an outgrowth of the student movement of the 1960s. Some social scientists, whose memories of that period are not especially fond, seem to fear that said teaching may be a front for ideological evangelization by radicals over thirty. There are hints of such fears in my sample of social scientists:

I do have misgivings about the formal teaching of ethics. . . . Many I know who are involved in the active practice of ethical teaching are people who seem to me tendentious and have an ideological focus to their work—they are not good mentors, even though they may be capable casuists (sociologist).

There is very little (teaching of ethics) except in the case of assorted leftists, who teach an ideologized ethics under the guise of social science (sociologist).

My sense is that this source of hostility to ethics is found mainly in sociology and anthropology, whereas concern about the unscientific nature of ethics is strongest in psychology.

Some social scientists, particularly those of a qualitative bent, also worry that instruction in ethics will reinforce the already strong trepidations of the timid. One prominent sociologist was quite explicit on this point:

> . . . there has been a lot of talk about field work, when it occurs in sociology, about the protection of human subjects. . . . If carried too far, students come to feel that there is nothing they can do which is not in some fashion immoral. . . . If students become too "pure," they will not stir—they will do library work or macro-cosmic things about domination and stratification, etc.

Another social scientist cited cases supporting this concern:

> Paradoxically, the system of Institutional Review Boards, mandated by the federal system to protect human subjects, has made graduate students skittish. They are anyway cautious about venturing off campus and fearful of interacting with strangers, and the elaborate system serves to rationalize their caution and encourage bookishness. In the past few years a number of promising students here have revised their dissertation proposals in order to have minimal contact with the local IRB (e.g., a student interested in the gay community ended by doing a content analysis of the gay press; a student interested in the female alcoholic now wants to study how women are viewed in various psychological testing instruments).

The nominal villain in these instances is the IRB, but the statement clearly implies that the teaching of ethics could reinforce the same propensity toward caution.

Finally, one social scientist who has taught in this field is concerned that ethics will become yet another isolated specialty in the social sciences, thus augmenting intellectual tendencies that are already lamentable.

> I dislike the emerging trend toward making ethics a specialized part of the curriculum and its teachers specialists in ethics. It accepts, and thus encourages, the deplorable evolution in the world of scholarship which sponsors it.

While hoping for a greater moral concern in the social sciences, this individual is highly critical of some who might promote it: " . . . every time I run into one of the new 'Ethicists' I retreat into a surly, destructive cynicism."

If wariness is the dominant attitude, sheer indifference is not far behind. As the following comments indicate, social scientists in several fields encountered neither opposition nor support from colleagues for their teaching efforts:

I have never heard it discussed among them—I suspect they would favor it, but are personally somewhat indifferent to it (anthropologist).

I cannot make a fair assessment of colleagues' attitudes except to say that ethics is seldom mentioned; and always in the context of fulfilling human subjects requirements. From this omission I will judge their attitudes to be indifferent or wary (psychologist).

I don't know how they would feel about classroom teaching—probably tolerant (social psychologist).

Others report an attitude that is seemingly supportive:

Generally at least mildly supportive in sociology. We've all taken Gouldner to heart concerning the need for more self-awareness. The numerous well-publicized abuses in social research have sensitized us to many of the main questions (sociologist).

. . . I sense no opposition among colleagues to any effort to link ethical concerns with instruction in research methodology. In fact, as the resistance of potential informants has become more serious with the great increase in the volume of social research, we all have been forced to think more seriously about ethics and reciprocity (sociologist).

Two social scientists who teach ethics at fairly small colleges even find their colleagues enthusiastic about their work. One commented:

Throughout the last ten years, my own colleagues have been extremely interested and supportive of the work I have done in the teaching of ethical issues in social science research. I have been encouraged to include this material in my own courses and have a number of colleagues with whom I have discussed these questions over the years (sociologist).

The other individual reported "consensual enthusiasm" about having a course on ethics in the catalogue.

Offsetting these positive cases are two others in which individuals concerned with ethics sense active hostility. In one department, the person in question taught a course on ethics, but was also active in local debates about the protection of human subjects. His comments suggest that the negative attitudes of his colleagues were directed much more at his stance on regulation than at his teaching:

> My sociology colleagues thought the *course* was a good idea although they were *violently* opposed to review of social science research proposals under the HEW/NIH guidelines. I found very little if any tacit agreement with my position favoring review and *no overt* support from my colleagues. I was verbally attacked by several colleagues for maintaining that social science research needs to be monitored for ethical propriety as does bio-medical research.

Another sociologist, who has written but not taught on the ethics of social science research, found the atmosphere at his university "indifferent to actively hostile." He stated that hostility is indicated by " . . . letters and statements saying local ethical peer review is not needed for social science."

Finally, a substantial number of social scientists seem to consider the teaching of ethics either irrelevant or uninteresting because there are no serious issues at stake. Adherents of this view generally advance one or both of the following arguments. First, the ethical questions raised by the social sciences, such as informed consent, intrusiveness, and harm to subjects, are of such slight moral import that they do not deserve much attention in teaching. A prominent psychologist seemed to take this position in a long letter to me on the teaching of ethics:

> Most students have overheard some discussion of "invasion of privacy" or "intrusiveness" of research procedures, and even more have encountered the issue of "confidentiality" of research data. At the same time, there is some interest in but less awareness of the issue of informed consent and the activities of IRB's. These questions arise principally in connection with questionnaire data and an occasional observational procedure. It has not been my experience that they raise serious, disturbing, or even interesting dilemmas.

He concludes that the moral dilemmas encountered are "relatively slight" and much less serious than in medicine and other fields.

The second argument is that even where there are legitimate areas of concern, the questions raised can often be handled more effectively by careful research than by philosophical reasoning. Thus, in evaluating the ethics of the Milgram obedience experiments, the best strategy is to conduct careful research on the effects of the research on the participants. The individual last quoted remarked in this connection:

> I happen to think that the question of "intrusiveness" of research procedures is one of the most interesting aspects of current ethical debates, though I regard it as an empirical rather than a moral question and one on which it is possible to do a certain amount of interesting research. Furthermore, the limited evidence suggests we know almost nothing about what subjects of research studies regard as intrusive. The basis for judging intrusiveness or invasion of privacy is highly subjective, terribly variable from individual to individual . . . and very badly in need of codification. Even when critics of social research appear to achieve consensus on the objectionability of a procedure—e.g., the Milgram obedience experiment—the evidence from observation of participants in the experiment does not seem to sustain their concern.

Ethical questions, in short, often boil down to testable hypotheses about consequences, in which case, much of the debate about the morality of research can be handled by research itself. This argument, of course, begs the question of the moral calculus to be used in assigning weights to consequences within a utilitarian framework, and basically denies the possibility of a deontological approach to such questions as lying. But it is a line of reasoning sometimes heard and more often held by social scientists trained in an ethos of positivism.

Another way to approach attitudes toward teaching is to ask how this and allied activities are rewarded in the various professions. In most departments, a social scientist whose published work was mainly on ethics would neither be rewarded nor penalized for this line of scholarship. A case in point is a young scholar who has written extensively on ethical aspects of the social sciences and who is slated for tenure review:

> . . . the department chairman told me that this (writing) wouldn't help much. I don't think (it) will hurt my chances—it may help slightly just by showing that I'm active and productive. However, I doubt if it will hurt either. It is just that they will evaluate me on my scientific work, teaching, and theorizing.
>
> My current interests are along more traditional lines. . . . For one thing, I felt that I had better focus in on such an area and publish or I would likely lose my job.

A senior scholar at a major university came to essentially the same conclusion:

> I suppose the reward structure does de-emphasize research and writing on

ethical issues. A young scholar would probably have to do an exceptionally outstanding job in studies about ethics to gain promotion in a major social science department.

This view was confirmed almost across-the-board by respondents from leading departments of anthropology, psychology, and sociology. The only exception would be for actual research on topics of ethical import, such as moral development:

> The answer is "yes" if it means research on moral development, helping behavior, just deserts, and the like. If all the person did was to develop an ethical position—let us say that they write a book like Sissela Bok's *On Lying (sic)*—my colleagues would say that the person would be appropriate for a Philosophy Department but not a Sociology Department (sociologist).

> The work on ethics would have to be geared to empirical research to fit current reward structures. There is no reason, however, why significant research could not be done on ethical problems (psychologist).

The general sense of the comments, confirmed by my own experience in several departments, is that in the leading departments work on ethics per se would neither help nor hinder promotion, in some small departments it would be favorably regarded, and in hostile environments of any size it could count against the candidate. Reactions may also depend on the balance between ethics and other spheres of professional involvement. An anthropologist commented:

> In general, I suspect that an anthropologist who devoted his or her entire attention to the field of ethics would be considered as something less than a full member of the club. We are burdened in this sense by the feeling that anthropologists are most properly employed in exploring strange lifeways.

I also asked respondents whether the teaching of ethics was encouraged or hindered by departmental, faculty, and university administrations. The replies suggest that administrators have relatively little direct impact on this field. Several individuals noted that in a time of retrenchment it is difficult to convince department chairmen and deans of the need for new courses on subjects perceived as peripheral to the discipline or for new faculty to teach such courses. But the case has obviously been made in a few departments, and deans and even presidents have sometimes been among the strongest advocates for renewed attention to ethics in the curriculum. Overall, the attitude of administrators in the universities covered here seems neither for nor against the teaching of ethics in the social sciences.

Student reactions appear generally positive, but not as much an energizer of teaching as a decade ago. In the leading graduate programs, students rarely press for courses or sections of courses on ethics, but appear interested when the topic is raised in class. Several commentators noted a drop in interest since the 1960s, whereas others reported an increase. My reading is that there is now less of a preoccupation with the sociopolitical aspects of ethics highlighted by the student movement, and more of a concern with such questions as the protection of human subjects and the ethics of applied research.

Two respondents also felt that exposure to ethical reflection can be confusing to graduate students, particularly when the discussions touch points of controversy within the profession:

> My students (in a course on ethics and the social sciences) were generally enthusiastic, but perplexed about how they could be both "ethical" and "successful" social scientists. Some of them were *pressured heavily* by faculty *not* to conform to the (university) requirements for review of dissertation research . . . (sociologist).

> Students are concerned about ethics, but need guidance and assistance. They especially tend to get confused and misdirected by the barrage of criticism of the social-scientific disciplines which is politically motivated and often factually wrong (e.g., that anthropologists were handmaidens of colonialism), when the true facts are far more complex and interesting (anthropologist).

Most instructors find that undergraduates, particularly those in introductory courses, have little sense of what constitutes an ethical issue, but quickly become interested as they are exposed to cases and commentary. Graduate student concern also seems to rise as individuals enter concrete research situations, and especially fieldwork, with all of the ethical dilemmas typically involved.

V. Whither the Teaching of Ethics?

The teaching of ethics has arrived, after a fashion, but its position is rather like that of a Piper Comanche at O'Hare Airport. It is indeed an aircraft, it comes on the runway with larger craft, and it is taken seriously by the control tower. At the same time it is dwarfed by the 747s, it is noticed by very few, and among those who do notice there is some sentiment that it should not be mixing with the commercial traffic. The question, then, is where the teaching of ethics will and should go from here. Should there be more explicit teaching about ethics? If so, what should be taught, how, and by whom?

Given the particular sample with which I began, it is not surprising that almost all of the respondents who chose to comment on the subject favored more teaching of ethics. Even so, one sociologist was frankly suspicious about this endeavor. In answer to a question about whether there should be more, less, or the same amount of teaching about ethical issues, he wrote:

> I don't know. I'm deeply suspicious of what would probably pass as "teaching about ethical issues," so perhaps the *status quo* is not so bad. The classroom is not a plausible locale for moral instruction.

Another sociologist who was sympathetic to the teaching of ethics, and had himself engaged in such teaching, questioned whether it would have any impact on behavior:

> On the one hand, research practice in social science is unethical both in its treatment of the people it studies and the systematic violation of methodological rules; on the other, I doubt that classroom discussion of ethics would make much of a dent.

A third sociologist expressed a different reservation: "More. But it must be informed philosophically lest it be folk ethics masquerading in the guise of social scientific legitimacy."

The specific reasons given in support of more teaching varied considerably. The following were two general statements:

> Because students want and need it. If students are prepared for the ethical (as well as methodological) difficulties they are going to encounter, they'll do better work. They'll also feel better about their work and themselves, and their relationship with those studied. Since the relationship between fieldworker and host people *is* the method, unlike other types of research where it merely influences the method, anything that improves the quality of the relationship may well improve the quality of the work (anthropologist).

> To be intelligent consumers and supporters of science, students need to learn how to evaluate what a scientist may and may not be allowed to do in the name of science. And, to be a morally good scientist, the student needs to understand how social contexts give rise to value conflicts between science and other interests and how these conflicts can be examined and equitable relationships between science and other institutions can be created (psychologist).

An eminent sociologist wrote that "it would probably be a good thing if professors gave more attention to ethical issues in their teaching. I think this will happen perhaps not so much from moral impulses as from practical necessity, as people out there that we study become ever more sophisticated about social research and concerned about what they should expect from researchers." But pragmatism was not the only theme expressed in these replies. One sociologist said very simply that ethics is "an intellectually and morally attractive subject."

If there should be greater teaching of ethics, what should be taught? Commentators from all of the disciplines stressed the need for discussions organized around concrete research cases, sometimes with, sometimes without broader ethical theory:

> I think general statements of ethical principles are of little value. I think students could learn a great deal from examining concrete cases where social scientists have encountered ethical problems and have dealt with those problems (sociologist).

> It should explore ethical dilemmas in contemporary social science research (using the case method) and teach ethical theory so that the student can develop the intellectual tools needed for analysis of contemporary problems. It should also explore larger questions about the role of science in society (psychology).

> Confrontations with issues, and wherever possible, guided field work. The

last because discussions of problems in which they are intimately involved gets to them much faster (anthropologist).

Others had specific suggestions for the content of courses, or parts of courses:

I expect that one of the expanding areas of social science during the 1980s will be policy and/or evaluation research. . . . We should always ask what are the ethical implications of doing research for any agency, public or private. It would be too easy to train students to do anything for a price (sociologist).

More consciousness-raising is needed to counteract the value-free myth and protect both subjects and researchers and the real values of science (psychologist).

Not only should ethics be considered as a regular topic, the specific application to the specific subject area should be specified. Just like the experimental method is reviewed in most classes as a guideline to ways of doing things, ethics should be given as a framework to judge what exists and plan the future (psychologist).

Another social scientist recommended "more attention to discriminating between critical problems and red herrings, more attention to concrete proposals and to the resolution of problems." Unfortunately, he did not define what he meant by "red herring."

From my perspective the only real surprise in these responses was the strength of sentiment about *how* ethics should be taught in the social sciences. The questionnaires contained long and sometimes impassioned statements about the need for integrating ethics into the regular social science curriculum and against making it into an esoteric and therefore professionally irrelevant sideshow. Several of these comments are worth quoting in detail:

I feel strongly that there should be well-integrated teaching of ethics in social sciences. I mean that ethical issues should not stand apart from the teaching of research methods and the establishment of priorities in social sciences generally. It would be a mistake, I believe, to see ethical issues as separable from substantive ones. This becomes particularly important when one turns to matters of policy research. . . . I am somewhat concerned that "ethics" might be taken as a separate issue from the conduct of social science considered more generally. I think developing ethical sensitivities in students and young researchers may not be done best by the development of insulated curricula (psychologist).

I think there ought to be more (teaching of ethics) although I'm not at all sure that a separate course on the subject makes sense. It ought to be incorporated into discussions of methods and research design—that is, given full recognition as one of the necessary areas to consider and analyze in carrying out a piece of research. . . like statistics, teaching on ethics is most likely to be absorbed if it comes up in the context of something that one is actively working on rather than taught as a separate, inevitably abstract set of issues (sociologist).

One individual is greatly concerned that the isolated teaching of ethics will not only be self-defeating, but will become part of the larger problem of intellectual fragmentation:

> I would like to see more scholar-teachers whose interest in their discipline extends beyond its boundaries to include the social context in which it exists; people who see themselves not simply as tradesmen or technicians (espousing psychology rather than plumbing), but as colleagues in a shared enterprise whose ultimate (unreachable) objective is truth. The difference between those who do and do not see their own work, and their field, as part of an integrated universe of knowledge is significant. The former cannot avoid, and the latter cannot recognize, the moral and ethical implications of what they do.
>
> It is not *additional* teaching that is needed, but teachers who, in their regular courses (Chem. I), proceed with an awareness of the moral freight their knowledge carries (psychologist).

Two respondents did recommend a separate course on ethics in the graduate curriculum. One felt that it should be required and should cover such issues as power, coercion, informed consent, and deception. At the same time this person, a psychologist, added that the teaching of ethics "really should be spread throughout all teaching as well as in a course. I try to bring it up throughout." A sociologist stated:

> I would argue for at least one formal course in the graduate curriculum. Attention should be given to ethical issues in social research, ethical implications of alternative theory construction strategies, positive responsibilities of social scientists. Attention to almost any issue would be better than what we are presently doing.

The gist of the comments is that ethics should be an integral part of teaching in the social sciences, rather than an appendage to the curriculum.

A. Recommendations

On the basis of this review, I would offer several specific recommendations for the teaching of ethics in the social sciences:
  1. *All social science departments should seek ways of introduc-*

ing students to the ethical dimensions of their disciplines. The day has passed when anthropology, psychology, sociology, and allied fields can be presented as if their subject matter, research methods, and practical applications raised no significant moral issues. If only as a matter of basic information and self-defense, students should be made aware that research and professional practice in the social sciences do raise ethical issues that are increasingly being monitored by outside agencies. More important, analysis of ethical issues in the social sciences can be an intellectually exciting endeavor that helps to set the disciplines themselves in their larger sociocultural and political context. Discussions of intrusiveness in social research, for example, are useful not only for alerting students to pitfalls and potential sources of embarrassment, but for considering the place of social research in contemporary society. In a course on sociology, it would be pedagogically interesting to examine social research as an institution and to ask how the values it serves, such as the generation of new information, mesh with other social values, such as privacy and autonomy. While the discussion of ethics will invariably lead to normative questions and usually judgments, the purpose of such teaching should not be the indoctrination of students into proper norms of professional behavior, but rather the analysis of critical moral issues arising in the relevant fields. Students should be given guiding concepts for identifying and specifying ethical issues and working principles for coming to practical conclusions, rather than a simple list of "do's" and "don'ts." The primary goal for the teaching of ethics, in other words, should be *education* about the ethical dimensions of the social sciences rather than catechesis in proper behavior. Where codes of ethics are available and pertinent, they can be discussed, but the teacher should always try to seek the principles behind such codes, rather than focus mainly on their prescriptions and prohibitions.

2. *The teaching of ethics should be integrated into all forms of teaching rather than confined to a separate course.* This does not mean that formal courses should be banned, but that the teaching of ethics should not be segregated into one corner of the curriculum. Instead, it should enter all the relevant kinds of teaching for a given field, including whole courses (where appropriate), sections of courses, informal discussions between faculty and stu-

dents, and such para-academic activities as colloquia and conferences. The danger with separate courses offered alone is that they can easily be perceived as a sop to ethics, a token effort to demonstrate concern but not a matter of serious professional interest. To be meaningful, ethics should enter what Henry James has called the "deep well of unconscious cerebration," and the teaching of ethics should be geared to that end. By this standard it is quite possible that departments with no formal courses on ethics, but with a deep commitment to ethics in other kinds of teaching, may have a greater impact on students than those where ethics is more in evidence, but penetrates less deeply.

3. *Graduate programs in the social sciences should offer a course devoted wholly or substantially to questions of ethics.* If faculty members are to have the background necessary to implement the previous recommendation, they will need systematic exposure to the relevant issues and literature. While self-instruction may be sufficient for some, in many cases teachers will need the preparation offered by a separate graduate course on ethics. Otherwise the "teaching of ethics" may become little more than raising a string of issues and then leaving them dangling before bewildered students who lack the tools to make sense of them. The suggested course need not, and perhaps should not, be confined to ethics. Given the close connections between ethical and political issues in these fields, a course on the ethics and politics of the social sciences might be both more stimulating and more intellectually valid than one dealing with ethics alone. While this course should be taken seriously, it should not be required, for required courses in the social sciences often carry the stigma of academic conscription and work against deep personal reflection on the issues raised.

4. *The teaching of ethics in the social sciences should normally be carried out by social scientists or by teams involving social scientists.* One simple reason for this recommendation is that almost no social science department in the United States has or will have the funds to hire a moral philosopher or theologian to "handle ethics." Given the choice between a member of the discipline with an interest in ethics and a philosopher with an interest in the discipline, few social science departments would opt for the latter. But the deepest reason for this suggestion goes

far beyond finances and recruitment preferences. As the earlier discussion suggests, it would be a pedagogical error to have teaching of ethics in the social sciences be primarily the responsibility of someone from outside those fields. If the goal of such teaching is not only to impart information and review conceptual frameworks, but to have students internalize a concern about the morality of their disciplines, it will not do to have the major instructors on ethics come from elsewhere. A philosopher or theologian might well conduct a superb seminar on the ethics of sociology, but such an individual would lack the credentials to become an effective role model for students about to enter that field. Unless the teacher were also a sociologist, he or she would not be equipped to advise graduate students on their dissertation research or discuss ethical issues informally on a "live" research project. This situation, in turn, would create the impression that ethics is really extraneous to sociology, a castor oil that one takes to become a healthy professional, but not an integral part of teaching, research, and professional practice. Indeed, to isolate ethics from the mainstream of professional training in the social sciences, and particularly from the informal instruction and role-modeling that lie at the heart of graduate training, might be worse than to have no formal instruction at all. At best it would lead to a compartmentalized approach to ethics, at worst to death by partial incorporation.

5. *Social scientists who engage in the teaching of ethics should have training in ethics suitable to the teaching in question.* There is clearly a difference in the amount of preparation required to conduct a full course in ethics in the social sciences and one class about ethics in a seminar on research methods. To avoid superficiality, with all its costs for the image of ethics, those offering separate course should be well-versed in the literature dealing specifically with ethics and the social sciences and also literate in moral philosophy. This literacy can be obtained in various ways, among them formal training in philosophy or theology, reading, and attending intensive seminars on ethics. Whatever the means, social scientists making a major commitment to the teaching of ethics should make a comparable commitment to developing the necessary intellectual skills for teaching. It will serve no one, least of all students, to have slapdash courses

taught by well-intentioned but ill-prepared instructors. As a minimum, social scientists offering courses on ethics should be able to make appropriate philosophical distinctions and to bring principles to bear on the issues raised. Those whose goal in teaching is mainly to sensitize students to ethical issues might be adequately prepared by a well-taught graduate seminar of the kind recommended earlier. The point of this proposal is not to advocate rigid credentials for the teaching of ethics, but to urge that social scientists who take up this challenge have the tools necessary to be effective teachers.

6. *Organizations specializing in applied ethics should sponsor short courses designed to assist social scientists in the teaching of ethics.* Institutions such as The Hastings Center and the Kennedy Institute of Bioethics at Georgetown University might experiment with brief courses specifically designed to meet the needs of social scientists interested in the teaching of ethics. Such courses should probably devote most of their attention to ethical frameworks, for this is an area in which most social scientists have little training. At the same time serious efforts could be made to link such frameworks to the ethical questions of greatest concern in the social sciences, such as deception, invasion of privacy, informed consent, and harm to participants in research.

7. *A serious effort should be made to improve the quality of the literature available for the teaching of ethics in the social sciences.* There is now a substantial literature on ethical issues in the social sciences, much of it concentrating on the ethics of research and of applications. Overall, the strength of this literature lies in the identification of ethical issues. Its pages are punctuated with statements such as "this raises a basic question of ethics" or "this research design is ethically suspect." The paramount weakness of this material is its inattention to basic philosophical distinctions and to ethical principles. For example, a recent book entitled *Ethics in Social and Behavioral Research* (see subsequent bibliography) provides an excellent overview on such topics as deception, privacy, informed consent, and risks to subjects, but gives the student little help with frameworks and principles for conceptualizing and resolving ethical dilemmas. At the same time philosophers and theologians have not been especially helpful in relating their frameworks specifically to the

ethical issues of greatest salience for the social sciences. Sissela Bok's book, *Lying*, is a notable exception, for it not only provides a general set of perspectives and principles for dealing with deception, but specifically addresses the question of lying in social research. It would be particularly useful at this stage to have one or more texts combining cases raising significant ethical questions with commentaries addressing those questions from the perspective of moral philosophy. Until the quality of the teaching materials is improved, even the best designed courses will suffer from the needless disjunction between issues and frameworks. This limitation applies to the materials in the next section, which are relatively weak on philosophical analysis.

VI. Topics and Readings

It would be fitting to conclude an essay on the teaching of ethics with a small contribution to teaching. To give a concrete sense of the material that might be covered in instruction on ethics in the social sciences, this last section will list several possible topics, together with appropriate readings.[23] The latter are illustrative rather than exhaustive, and are themselves a source for other material. The general works which I have found particularly useful include:

Bower, R.T. and de Gasparis, P. *Ethics in Social Research: Protecting the Interests of Human Subjects.* New York: Praeger, 1978.

Callahan, D. and Bok Sissela, eds. *Ethics Teaching in Higher Education.* New York, Plenum Press, 1980.

Diener, E. and Crandall, R., *Ethics in Social and Behavioral Research.* Chicago: University of Chicago Press, 1978.

Katz, J., *Experimentation with Human Beings: The Authority of the Investigator, Subject, Professions, and State in the Human Experimentation Process.* New York: Russell Sage Foundation, 1972.

Kelman, H., *A Time to Speak: On Human Values and Social Research.* San Francisco: Jossey-Bass, 1968.

Reich, W.T., ed. *Encyclopedia of Bioethics,* New York and London: The Free Press and Collier Macmillan, 1978, 4 vols.

Sjoberg, G., ed. *Ethics, Politics, and Social Research.* Cambridge, Mass.: Schenkman Publishing Company, 1967.

The Teaching of Ethics in Higher Education: A Report by The Hastings Center. Hastings-on-Hudson, N.Y.: The Hastings Center, 1980.

A. Social Science and Society

1. *Social science as a reflection and expression of ethical values.*
   How is social science affected by the surrounding society in
   general and by shared ethical values in particular? To what
   extent, and in what ways, do the social sciences derive their
   manifest and latent ethics from the larger ethos in which they
   find themselves? Can social science be "value free?" What is
   the meaning of "objectivity" in these fields?

Diener and Crandall, chap. 12.

Friedrichs, R.W., *A Sociology of Sociology.* New York: The Free Press, 1970.

Gouldner, A., "Anti-Minotaur: The Myth of Value-Free Sociology." *Social
    Problems 9* (1962): 199–213.

MacRae, D., Jr. *The Social Function of Social Science.* New Haven: Yale Uni-
    versity Press, 1976, chaps. 1–3.

2. *Social science as a source of ethical values.* What effect do
   the assumptions, conceptualizations, research procedures, and
   findings of the social sciences have on the ethics of the larger
   society? Do they encourage certain notions of right and
   wrong, of the tolerable and the intolerable, of the normal and
   the deviant? What impact, if any, do latent assumptions about
   human nature, such as those built into psychoanalytic theory,
   have on individual and collective conceptions of morality?

Bauer, R.A., *The New Man in Soviet Psychology.* Cambridge, Mass.: Harvard
    University Press, 1952.

Friedrichs. *A Sociology of Sociology,* chaps. 2, 3, 6, 8.

Kelman, chap. 1.

Rieff, P., *The Triumph of the Therapeutic: Uses of Faith After Freud.* New
    York: Harper and Row, 1966.

Seeley, J., *The Americanization of the Unconscious.* New York: Science House,
    1967, chaps. 1, 7.

3. *Social science, ethics, and the distribution of power.* Do the
   theories or research findings of social science give power ad-
   vantages to some segments of society at the expense of others? Do these disciplines generally promote or inhibit social

change? How should social scientists relate themselves to the power issues involved in their work?

Diener and Crandall, chap. 13.

Kelman, chap. 2.

M. Nicolaus, "Remarks at ASA Convention." *American Sociologist* 4:2 (1969): 154–56. See also reply by Richard Robbins, pp. 156–58.

B. Generic Ethical Issues in Social Research

1. *Truth-telling and deception.* Is it ever justifiable for the social scientist to engage in deception or misrepresentation for such ends as improved data-collection or the welfare of exploited groups? What standards of truth-telling should prevail in the reporting of social scientific findings?

Bok, Sissela. *Lying: Moral Choice in Public and Private Life.* New York: Pantheon Books, 1978, esp. chaps. 1–3, 11.

Diener and Crandall, chap. 5.

Douglas, J.D., *Investigative Social Research: Individual and Team Field Research.* Beverly Hills: Sage Publications, 1976, chaps. 1, 4.

Kelman, chap. 8.

2. *Privacy.* What are the ethical limits on intrusion in social scientific research? Do communities as well as organizations have an ethical claim to privacy? What are the obligations of the social scientist to protect the privacy of data once they are collected, e.g., if there is a subpoena?

Diener and Crandall, chap. 4.

Greenawalt, Kent. "Privacy," in *Encyclopedia of Bioethics.*

Ruebhausen, O.M. and Brim, O.G., Jr. "Privacy and Behavioral Research." *Columbia Law Review* 65 (1965): 1184–1211.

3. *Informed Consent.* Do participants or subjects in social scientific research have the right to informed consent? Are there some types of situations, such as observation in public places or even field research in communities, where the requirement of prior consent is not necessary or virtually meaningless? What ethical problems are posed when the potential partici-

pants in research, such as the very poor or those with mental
disorders, lack the capacity fully to understand the nature and
consequences of research?

Diener and Crandall, chap. 3.

Articles on "Informed Consent in Human Research" by Bradford Gray and by
Karen Lebacqz and Robert J. Levine. *Encyclopedia of Bioethics.*

4. *Risk, benefit, and human welfare.* What ethical framework
should be applied in evaluating the impact of social scientific
research on individuals and groups? Is the risk/benefit approach, which derives from the utilitarian tradition in ethics,
the most appropriate model? Are there some harms to participants that are never justifiable, however great the putative
benefits for science? Whose frameworks, and whose weighting
of the values at stake, should prevail when there are likely to
be differences in the criteria of welfare applied by the researcher and those studied?

Barber, B. "Some Perspectives on the Role of Assessment of Risk/Benefit Criteria in the Determination of the Appropriateness of Research Involving Human Subjects." Paper prepared for the National Commission for
the Protection of Human Subjects of Biomedical and Behavioral Research. Bethesda, Md.: U.S. Department of Health, Education, and
Welfare, 1975.

Childress, J.F. "Risk." In *Encyclopedia of Bioethics.*

Diener and Crandall, chap. 2.

Kelman, H. "Behavioral Research." In *Encyclopedia of Bioethics.*

C. Ethical Issues Arising from Specific Research Methods and Settings

1. *Laboratory experiments.* What are the major forms of potential harm for participants in laboratory studies? Is deception
ethically acceptable in these settings? Is deception here different from deception elsewhere? What are the power relations
between researchers and researched in the laboratory? Can
these be equalized without damage to the scientific value of
the research?

Baumrind, D., "Some Thoughts on Ethics of Research: After Reading Milgram's 'Behavioral Study of Obedience'." *American Psychologist 19* (1964): 421–23.

Katz, J., *Experimentation with Human Beings,* sections on laboratory experiments.

Kelman, H. "The Rights of the Subject in Social Research: An Analysis in Terms of Relative Power and Legitimacy." *American Psychologist 27* (1972): 989–1016.

Milgram, S. *Obedience to Authority: An Experimental View.* New York: Harper and Row, 1974.

2. *Open field observation.* This method refers to field work in which the observer is openly identified as a researcher and does not engage in deception or misrepresentation about the nature of the research. What ethical issues arise with the observational techniques commonly used by social anthropologists and qualitative sociologists? How well, if at all, does the paradigm of informed consent and other subject protections developed for laboratory research apply to field settings? If this paradigm is inappropriate, what are the alternatives?

Cassell, J. "Risk and Benefit to Subjects of Fieldwork." *American Sociologist* 13:3 (1978) 134–43.

Rynkiewich, M.A. and Spradley, J.P. *Ethics and Anthropology: Dilemmas in Fieldwork.* New York: John Wiley and Sons, 1976.

Wax, M. "On Fieldworkers and Those Exposed to Fieldwork: Federal Regulations and Moral Issues." *Human Organization 36* (1977): 321–28.

Weaver, T., ed. *To See Ourselves: Anthropology and Modern Social Issues.* Glenview, Ill.: Scott, Foresman, and Company, 1973. See especially chapter by G. Berreman on "The Social Responsibility of the Anthropologist," pp. 5–61.

3. *Covert observation.* Do social scientists ever have the right to engage in research by posing as members of groups to which they do not really belong (Festinger et al.), acting as "pseudopatients" to observe hospitals (Rosenhan) or becoming an accomplice in illegal activities (Humphreys)? Do the ends of social research, such as improving the lot of homosexuals or exposing the insanity of mental hospitals, ever justify deception and misrepresentation in the research process?

Diener and Crandall, chap. 7.

Festinger, L., Riecken, H., and Schachter, S. *When Prophecy Fails.* Minneapolis: University of Minnesota Press, 1956.

Humphreys, L. *Tearoom Trade: Impersonal Sex in Public Places* (enlarged ed.). Chicago: Aldine Publishing Company, 1975.

Rosenhan, D.L. "On Being Sane in Insane Places." *Science* 179 (1973): 250–58.

Warwick, D. "Tearoom Trade: Means and Ends in Social Research." *Hastings Center Studies,* 1:1 (1973): 27–38 (also reprinted in Humphreys).

4. *Survey research: polls, market research, and other surveys.* What are the most significant ethical issues raised by surveys? Is it ever ethically accepable, as in a private poll for a candidate, to slant the sample or otherwise make the study come out with the "right" results? Given the need for relatively quick explanations to gain the cooperation of respondents at the door, how much information about the purpose and contents of the survey is required for informed consent? What steps should be taken to protect the confidentiality of survey data?

Bogart, L. *Silent Politics: Polls and the Awareness of Public Opinion.* New York: Wiley-Interscience, 1972.

Cain, L.D., Jr. "The AMA and the Gerontologists: Uses and Abuses of 'A Profile of the Aging: USA'." In Sjoberg, pp. 78–114.

King, A.J. and Spector, A.J. "Ethical and Legal Aspects of Survey Research." *American Psychologist 18* (1963): 204–5.

Warwick, D. and Lininger, C. *The Sample Survey: Theory and Practice.* New York: McGraw-Hill Book Company, 1975, chap. 8 (for an explanation of how a survey interview is typically conducted).

5. *Social experiments.* In recent years the United States government has sponsored a number of experiments to test the viability of policies such as income maintenance. They typically involve a combination of research methods, including repeated surveys. Should the design of social experiments reflect the values and preferences only of the government, or should the options preferred by others be included? Should

participants be protected against the boon of certain benefits, such as extra income, when their acceptance may produce long-term harm? If individuals suffer losses as a result of the experiment, do its organizers have any obligation to restore the status quo ante?

Rivlin, A.M. and Timpane, M.P., eds. *Ethical and Legal Issues of Social Experimentation.* Washington: Brookings Institution, 1975.

Rossi, P., Boeckmann, M. and Berk, R. "Some Ethical Implications of the New Jersey-Pennsylvania Income Maintenance Experiment," in G. Bermant, H. Kelman, and D. Warwick, eds. *The Ethics of Social Intervention.* Washington, D.C.: Hemisphere Publishing Company, 1978, pp. 245–66.

Warwick, D. "Ethical Guidelines for Social Experiments." In ibid., pp. 267–88.

6. *Crosscultural research.* Are there any unique ethical issues arising in research crossing national or cultural boundaries? Are these more serious when the researcher is a member of a dominant group and is studying those with less power, or comes from a relatively wealthy nation to carry out research with local collaborators possessing few resources? Should social scientists engage in crossnational studies that are sponsored by military or intelligence agencies? What are the lessons of Project Camelot? (Note: some of these issues are covered in part by the readings in the section on open field observation).

Adams, R.N. "Responsibility of the Foreign Scholar to the Local Scholarly Community." *Current Anthropology* 12:3 (1971): 335–39.

Beals, R. *Politics of Social Research.* Chicago: Aldine Publishing Company, 1969.

Kelman, chap. 3.

Tapp, J.L., Kelman, H.C., Triandis, H.C., Wrightsman, L.S., and Coelho, G.V. "Continuing Concerns in Cross-Cultural Ethics: A Report." *International Journal of Psychology* 9 (1974): 231–49.

Warwick, D. "The Politics and Ethics of Cross-Cultural Research." In H.C. Triandis, W.W. Lambert, and J.W. Berry, eds. *Handbook of Cross-Cultural Psychology,* vol. I. Boston: Allyn and Bacon, 1979.

D. Applied Social Science and the Ethics of Intervention

The question of the ethics of applied work arises in all of the social science disciplines. For whom should one work? What constraints should be accepted? When consulting or other applied social science is likely to affect the balance of power in a community, an organization, or other unit, does the social scientist have an ethical responsibility to those whose leverage will be reduced? Should social science skills be open to the highest bidder, or should consideration of justice enter into the question? This is a vast topic in which the specific ethical questions vary greatly by discipline and setting. The ethical aspects of applied anthropology are discussed quite regularly in the pages of *Human Organization*. Related discussions can be found in the *Journal of Applied Behavioral Science,* the *American Sociologist,* and the *American Psychologist.* A recent work which deals with the ethics of applications and interventions in several settings is:

Bermant, G., Kelman, H., and Warwick, D., eds. *The Ethics of Social Intervention.* Washington, D.C.: Hemisphere Publishing Company (Wiley/Halsted), 1978.

The book contains pairs of articles, and often extensive bibliography, on: behavior control, encounter groups, organization development, consulting activities (housing and education programs), crisis interventions, social experiments, and international population programs. Students interested in this general area would be well advised to select one particular sphere of applied activities, such as behavior modification, for detailed analysis.

Notes

1. I committed this error in a preliminary article on the teaching of ethics in the social sciences (*Hastings Center Report*, December, 1977). My estimate of the number of courses offered proved quite accurate, but I seriously underestimated the total amount of teaching by concentrating only on formal courses.

2. G. Sjoberg, ed., *Ethics, Politics, and Social Research* (Cambridge, Mass.: Schenkman Publishing Company, 1967).

3. H. Kelman, *A Time to Speak: On Human Values and Social Research* (San Francisco: Jossey-Bass, 1968).

4. I offered such a course at York University in Toronto in the spring of 1972, and it proved disastrous. Of the five students who appeared for the first sessions, three had no conception of ethics, one had some special political concerns, and one was generally confused about the entire set of issues. This was surprising to me in light of the very successful experience Herbert Kelman and I had had with a similar course offered at Harvard three years before.

5. J. Katz, ed., *Experimentation with Human Beings* (New York: Russell Sage Foundation, 1972).

6. M. Glazer, *The Research Adventure* (New York: Random House, 1972).

7. Reply to questionnaire on the teaching of ethics.

8. Cf. S.L. Warner, "Randomized response: A survey technique for eliminating evasive answer bias," *Journal of the American Statistical Association* 60 (1965): 63–69.

9. A.J. Vidich and J. Bensman, *Small Town in Mass Society (rev. ed.)* (Princeton: Princeton University Press, 1968). See also "Freedom and Responsibility in Research: The Springdale Case," *Human Organization* 16 (1958): 1–2.

10. H. Dobyns, P.L. Doughty, and H. Lasswell. *Peasants, Power, and Applied Social Change: Vicos as a Model* (Beverly Hills: Sage Publishing Company, 1964).

11. C.N. Turnbull, *The Mountain People* (New York: Simon and Schuster, 1972); F. Barth, "On Responsibility to Humanity," *Current Anthropology 15* (1974): 99–102.

12. M.L. Wax and J. Cassell, eds., *Federal Regulations: Ethical Issues and Social Research* (Boulder, Colorado: Westview Press, 1979).

13. *The Teaching of Ethics in Higher Education: A Report by The Hastings Center* (Hastings-on-Hudson, N.Y.: The Hastings Center, 1980).

14. S. Milgram, *Obedience to Authority: An Experimental View* (New York: Harper and Row, 1974); I.L. Horowitz, ed., *The Rise and Fall of Project Camelot* (Cambridge, Mass.: MIT Press, 1967); L. Humphreys, *Tearoom Trade* (rev. ed.) (Chicago: Aldine, 1975).

15. R.W. Friedrichs, *A Sociology of Sociology* (New York: The Free Press, 1970), p. 94.

16. C.T. Morgan and R.A. King, *Introduction to Psychology* (New York: McGraw-Hill, 1966).

17. R.L. Sutherland, J.L. Woodward, and M.A. Maxwell, *Introductory Sociology* (Chicago: J. Lippincott Company, 1961).

18. Cf. M. Weber, *Methodology of the Social Sciences,* trans. and ed. by E.A. Shils and H.A. Finch (Glencoe, Illinois: The Free Press, 1949), esp. pp. 49–112.

19. Friedrichs, *A Sociology . . . ,* p. 81.

20. Quoted in ibid., pp. 94–95.

21. M. Nicolaus, "Remarks at ASA Convention," *American Sociologist* 4:2 (1969): 155.

22. Books on Project Camelot include I.L. Horowitz, *The Rise and Fall . . . ,* and R.L. Beals, *Politics of Social Research* (Chicago: Aldine Publishing Company, 1969). The volume by Beals begins with Project Camelot and then moves on to consider broader issues of politics and ethics in international research by American social scientists.

23. The following outline builds on the syllabus used in the course on ethics taught by Herbert Kelman and myself at Harvard University in 1969–70.

Appendix A

Questionnaire on the Teaching of Ethics in the Social Sciences

1. Have you personally been at all involved in the teaching of ethics in the social sciences, whether formally and explicitly or more informally (e.g., encouraging students to think about the moral dimensions of social research without giving formal lectures on research ethics)? If so, could you indicate the nature and extent of your involvement.

    1a. (*If Personally Involved*) How did you happen to become interested in the teaching of ethics?

2. From what you can see in your own and related disciplines, how extensive is the teaching of ethics in the social sciences? What forms does this teaching take? Please cite any illustrations you can think of.

3. How would you characterize the attitudes of your professional colleagues toward the teaching of ethics? Are they enthusiastic, mildy supportive, tolerant or indifferent, wary, or hostile? Cite any specifics illustrating or supporting your judgment.

4. How about student attitudes toward the teaching of ethics? Is there student pressure for greater attention to ethical concerns and, if so, in what quarters of the student body? Have you noticed any change in student attitudes over, say, the past decade?

5. Do you feel there should be more, less, or about the same amount of teaching about ethical issues in the social sciences? Why?

    5a. (*If More*) What, form should additional teaching take? What issues should receive the greatest attention?

    5b. (*If Less*) What, specifically, do you think should be deemphasized?

6. At the level of departmental, faculty, or university administration, are there any significant obstacles to the teaching of ethics? Any significant pressures or sources of support?

7. How about the reward structure of the social science disciplines—does it encourage or discourage the teaching of ethics, or have no impact? In your own field would it be possible for a younger scholar to be given tenure in a major department if his/her work were of high quality but concentrated entirely in the field of ethics?

8. Do you know of social scientists at your own institution or others with significant interests in the ethical aspects of the social sciences? If so, could you indicate their names and institutions so that we can contact them.

9. If you are teaching or have taught a course which deals explicitly with ethical questions, including one in which ethics is but one part, could you please send along a copy of your most recent syllabus.

10. Do you have any other comments on the general subject of teaching ethics in the social sciences?

Appendix B

Persons Contacted

The following individuals either completed the questionnaire included in Appendix A or provided information relevant to this essay by letter or telephone. Their cooperation is gratefully acknowledged and much appreciated.

Richard Adams
Department of Anthropology
University of Texas
Austin, TX 78712

Bernard Barber
Department of Sociology
Barnard College
Columbia University
New York, NY 10522

Peter Berger
Department of Sociology
Rutgers University
New Brunswick, NJ 08903

Gordon Bermant
The Federal Judicial Center
Dolly Madison House
1520 "H" St., N.W.
Washington, D.C. 20005

Robert Boruch
Department of Psychology
Northwestern University
Evanston, IL 60201

Sidney Callahan
Department of Psychology
Fairfield University
Fairfield, CT 06430

Angus Campbell
Survey Research Center
Institute for Social Research
Ann Arbor, MI 48104

Donald T. Campbell
Department of Psychology
Northwestern University
Evanston, IL 60201

Joan Cassell
Center for Policy Research
New York, NY

Erve Chambers
Dept. of Anthropology
College of Social and Behavioral
  Sciences
University of South Florida
Tampa, Florida 33620

Rick Crandall
Institute of Behavioral Research
Texas Christian University
Fort Worth, TX 76129

William V. D'Antonio
Department of Sociology
University of Connecticut
Storrs, CT 06268

Edward Diener
Department of Psychology
University of Illinois
Champaign, IL 61820

Robert W. Friedrichs
Department of Sociology
Williams College
Williamstown, MA 01267

John Galliher
Department of Sociology
University of Missouri
Columbia, MO 65201

William Gamson
Department of Sociology
University of Michigan
Ann Arbor, MI 48104

Angela B. Ginorio
Department of Psychology
Bowling Green State University
Bowling Green, OH 43403

Myron Glazer
Department of Sociology and
  Anthropology
Smith College
Northampton, MA 01063

Norman Hilmar
Department of Sociology
University of Colorado
Boulder, CO 80302

Daniel Katz
Department of Psychology
University of Michigan
Ann Arbor, MI 48104

Herbert C. Kelman
Department of Psychology and Social
  Relations
Harvard University
Cambridge, MA 02138

Charles Lidz
Department of Psychiatry
University of Pittsburgh
Pittsburgh, PA 15213

William Osborne
Department of Sociology and
  Anthropology
Florida International University
Tamiami Trail
Miami, FL 33199

E.L. Pattullo
Department of Psychology and Social
  Relations
Harvard University
Cambridge, MA 02138

Conrad Reining
Department of Anthropology
Catholic University of America
Washington, D.C. 20064

Henry W. Riecken
Professor of Behavioral Science
The School of Medicine
University of Pennsylvania
Philadelphia, PA. 19104

David Riesman
Department of Sociology
Harvard University
Cambridge, MA 02138

Joan Sieber
Department of Psychology
California State University at
  Hayward
Hayward, CA 94542

Robert Textor
Department of Anthropology
Stanford University
Stanford, CA 94305

Michael Useem
Department of Sociology
Boston University
Boston, MA 02215

Ted Vaughan
Department of Sociology
University of Missouri
Columbia, MO 65201

Murray Wax
Department of Sociology and
  Anthropology
Washington University
St. Louis, MO 63130

Andrew Weigert
Department of Sociology and
  Anthropology
University of Notre Dame
Notre Dame, IN 46556

William Foote Whyte
New York State School of Industrial
  and Labor Relations
Cornell University
Ithaca, NY 14853

Everett K. Wilson
Department of Sociology
University of North Carolina
Chapel Hill, NC 27514